T0366940

*Hysterical Water*

Georgia Review Books *Edited by Gerald Maa*

# *Hysterical Water*

*Poems*

HANNAH BAKER SALTMARSH

The University of Georgia Press *Athens*

Published by the University of Georgia Press
Athens, Georgia 30602
www.ugapress.org

Designed by Erin Kirk
Set in Arno
Printed and bound by Sheridan Books
The paper in this book meets the guidelines for permanence and durability of the Committee on Production Guidelines for Book Longevity of the Council on Library Resources.

Most University of Georgia Press titles are available from popular e-book vendors.

Printed in the United States of America
24 23 22 21 20 P 5 4 3 2 1

Library of Congress Control Number: 2020950825
ISBN: 9780820359007 (pbk.: alk. paper)
ISBN: 9780820359014 (ebook)

For Jay

& in Memory of Stanley Plumly (1939–2019)

*Hysteria, n.* Origin: A borrowing from Latin. Etymon: Latin *hysteria*. Compare French *hystérie*, syndrome affecting women, extreme excitement or agitation. Hysteria was originally thought to be due to a disturbance of the uterus and its functions; compare the German term *Mutterweh*. Originally: a (supposed) physical disorder characterized by neurological symptoms (such as an inability to perform voluntary movements, loss of vision or hearing, seizure-like episodes, etc.), often accompanied by exaggeratedly emotional behavior. The disorder attributed to the uterus was known earlier in English by names including *rising of the mother*, *suffocation of the mother*, and *hysteric passion* or *hysterical passion.*

*Hysterical, adj.* Of, relating to, or of the nature of the hysterical passion or hysteria. Used in the treatment of disorders of or attributed to the uterus, esp. the hysterical passion. In later use: exhibiting or inclined to extreme or unrestrained emotion; overwhelmed by emotion. Extremely funny, hilarious (colloq.).

—*Oxford English Dictionary*

Dora says:

"I knew *you'd* say that."

"I go to my room, not the slightest bit sad, and read a big book on my desk."

"I've asked you a hundred times where the key is."

"What satisfaction?"

"So what's really come out? . . . You do know, doctor, that this is the last time I'll be coming here?"

"How did they find the letter in the first place? After all, it was locked in my desk."

"Where is the station? I keep getting the same answer: five minutes away . . . there's that habitual feeling of anxiety that you have when you can't get any further in the dream."

"I can't think about anything else."

—an arrangement of selections from Sigmund Freud's *Fragment of an Analysis of a Case of Hysteria (Dora)*, 1905

# Contents

# Acknowledgments

My gratitude to the editors of the following journals in which poems from this collection first appeared: *Feminist Studies*; the *Keats-Shelley Review*; *ISLE: Interdisciplinary Studies in Literature*; *MOM Egg Review*; *Qualm*; *Hotel Amerika*; *Connotation Press*; the *American Poetry Review*; the *New Republic*; AGNI; *Prairie Schooner*; the *Kenyon Review*; *Maternal Journal/ Project for Empty Space*; the *Denver Quarterly*; and the *Birmingham Review*.

Thank you to the Oxford Publishing Limited for the usage of two definitions from the *Oxford English Dictionary*, "hysteria" and "hysterical," which are reproduced by permission of the licensor through PLSclear.

A short-term fellowship at the Folger Shakespeare Library in the summer of 2017 allowed me to explore archival material essential to this book. Special thanks to Dr. Amanda Herbert, associate director of fellowships, and to all of the scholars and artists who gathered in the Tea Room to share ideas and quandaries. Thank to the early modern women (some of whom are anonymous) whose work I read at the Folger, and who inspired "The Matrix Miscellany." A grant from the Maryland State Arts Council in 2019 provided me with resources to edit the book and write new poems.

To my UMD poetry professors and mentors whose voices I still hear whenever I write: Liz Arnold, Don Berger, Michael Collier, and Josh Weiner. I can't thank you enough for nourishing my creative life and for the idiosyncratic, invaluable ways in which you write, teach, and respond to poetry.

To Michael Olmert for modeling concision and mystery.

To Sheila Jelen for the writing lesson of a lifetime: finding a "punctum" in a poem like Barthes does in photography.

To the memory of Stanley Plumly; and to the integrity, affection, and gravitas of Plumly's dictum: "Just do the work and the rest will take care of itself."

To my writer friends and fellow creatives for feedback, support, and love: Sarah Antine, Lindsay Bernal, Sarah Beth Childers, Liz Countryman, K. D. Doyle, John Gery, Anya Groner, Sofi Hall, Biljana Obradović, Amanda Page, Kat DeBlassie Page, Amy Kurzweil, Meg Vesper, and Cocoa Williams.

To my parents and my three brothers for kindling a love of hyperbole, metaphor, humor, and storytelling. To my maternal and paternal grandparents for your stories and voices.

To my high school English teachers who conferenced with me about my terrible poems and entertained my relentless questions about what poets could have possibly meant.

To Reena Sastri for talking with me passionately about confessional poetry.

To my own former and current students for taking creative risks and asking questions. To my student L.K., who wants to write enough books that she can dedicate a different one to each of her many favorite humans.

To Gerald Maa for believing in this book and for editing it empathetically and honestly, for a friendship and collaboration across more than a decade, and for letters along the way.

To everyone at the University of Georgia Press, especially Thomas Roche and Beth Snead.

To Lenka Clayton for founding "An Artist's Residency in Motherhood" and for making child-friendly art exhibits and affirming the voices of mothers and their children in various creative projects. To Project for Empty Space and the *Maternal Journal* for bringing mother artists together in a kid-friendly fashion.

To my husband, Jay, for the time, support, love, and faith that has made a writing life with three young children possible. Thank you for the heat in the sun porch, and for believing in all my impractical pursuits. To my children, Juliet, Chadwick, and Scarlett, for your love of words, creative play, and closeness.

# 1.

## A Lady Author's Defense of the Female Sex, 1696

A bitch can learn as many tricks
in as little time as a dog.

I am done wondering on those men
who can write huge volumes on

slender subjects. A man who spends much
time writing, but ten times more

reading over what he's written. The Poetical
Haberdasher of Small Wares, love odes

and elegies. His pocket's an inexhaustible Magazine
of Rhymes and Nonsense. His tongue

a repeating clock with chimes.
The Plague of the Press, The Ruin

of the Bookseller. Men thus waste their fortunes
as well as their lives. If "a woman is a failed

man," St. Thomas Aquinas, there's no
better test in which to fail.

Sustained enrollment in school isn't the only
way to learn languages, spot a lunar rainbow,

compose verse when there's world
travel, the imagination, a garden, peculiar

people everywhere, women's company.
You don't know what I'm thinking of at the root

of four tongues I plan to bake and blanch
and rub well, but I have in the make and temper

of my womanly body proof that we were
not meant for fatigue or for statements

like "I have wasted my life," the male poet in
his hammock cradle on an untended farm (and not

his anyway, but William Duffy's)
might brag, important as Hamlet to be

bemoaning inaction. Some of us have work to do.
Places we have to, all the while dreaming, be.

## Index of Jobs for Women

I would have been a confectioner, not Shakespeare's sister,
whirring a dozen egg whites into soft collapsible peaks
for baked rice pudding with black-blue currants,
stirring yeasty sourdough starter a few times a day
until it ferments vigorously, more quickly in summer: a week
to evolve. I would have tried to find a way to the youngest son
who lives by the brackish waters, tall sea grasses, canals by crocodiles,
and sedges with their edges, whose heart is bigger than his head,
whose narrow bikeway of a torso might have said, on the last
day of the month, my rolls were his best meal in June.
My grandmother made yeast buns when she was sad.
Her other jobs—washer woman, dyer, doula, butcher, maid, madam,
weaver, wag, scribe of To-Do, coach, cobbler, apothecary, pedant, and
the soul of the place, alma mater, reverend mother, mother superior—
never made anyone as happy over her, with everyone close by, as baker.
But my grandmother was someone else, too: the prettiest wave,
stationed in Hawaii, one of the WAVES, and smarter than the man over her
who roared the wrong directive once, got sent home, a shameful discharge.
Not a white-gloved fingerprint of dust on her bedsprings at the daily inspection,
an oldest child. Jane in and out of the libraries; Jane the Poet Laureate
of Waikiki Beach before it was touristy, before we made it touristy.
Poet of the banyan tree, also shade to the island-goddess "wrinkled and little,
stringing purple orchids with a wooden needle." Jane outlives her leis
in the photograph, each drowsy surfer–hand gesture to the hoolah,
her ravished cigarettes imprinted with the kisses of World-War-II red lipstick,
her split-the-shin grass skirt: how she ran a farm before this,
surfacing through rambling fields, vines, rising creek, or cracking
a watermelon open in her lap like a book spine loosening,
acquiring its book scent as it tastes the era. Jane today always gets the drift
even with her hearing aids out, even half-asleep, answering the phone at ninety-nine,
or typing up the nursing home newsletter, editing everyone's columns,
smiling how her mother-in-law didn't want her son marrying a college girl.

## Lactivist Manifesto

*Prologue: To My Children*

My breast was in your mouth half the time when you were babies. You wanted to feed me too, your hand scraping up my chin. A while it's true you were inside of me longer than you were outside me living. I would gasp when you coughed, turned your head, hiccupped in your sleep.

What were you collecting inside yourselves, all three of my little ones who tried to swallow everything? What could have gone wrong with the mailbox key, the infinity-shaped back of an earring I don't even like or have the other one for, the boxy torso of a Lego woman, no head or hands? A white bead on the playground stair, the lid of the cinnamon, an acorn without its winter hat? Lenka Clayton's baby Otto tried to ingest the worst little pieces in hotel rooms, attics, the ground, and all around the world: a rat poison sachet being the worst, but then cigarette butts, beer bottle caps, a tough leaf. In the first ever childproof museum, photographs of sixty-three objects taken from Otto's mouth as if to mock the fear that never aided survival anyway. Now, Otto is seven: he collects mismatched keys and locks, also allied in his mother's museum.

My aunt telling me the days are long, the years are short. Everything is hard right now when everything is beautiful right now. The beads of my sweat hitting your mouth, half-open at the breast in breastmilk dreams.

*1.*

To Alicia Ostriker, breastfeeding is better than ardor, which is a "bitter honey" anyway. Ostriker celebrates in her baby, in herself, "the pleasure of touching / and being touched by this most perfect thing / this pear blossom." A way of being together beyond all the other forms of innocence.

2.

Know your rights: "A mother may breastfeed her baby or express breast milk in any location, public or private, where the mother is otherwise authorized to be. Furthermore, women seen in the act of breastfeeding will not be considered for 'indecent exposure, sexual conduct, lewd touching, or obscenity.'" Kentucky 122.755 (1). Yet, you will hear:

"I can't believe she is doing that in public."
"You might want to make sure a woman sits next to you so it's not awkward for everybody."
"You can't do that in the sanctuary. Maybe try somewhere private."
"That's too sexual; breasts are an arousing area: that's why I couldn't breastfeed."
"When are you going to wean her?!"
"In front of my husband?!"

None of my babies liked the nursing cover; the flurry of a blanket peaking with elbows, fists; the heat in the heat.

3.

A lactivist is a surrealist: jigsaw together a reclining baby, a tipped nipple, the entanglement of hands, the stopping and starting, intermittent dreaming, sleeping, demanding, the spastic calm, the fringes of eyelashes like flapper bangs.

4.

Messages my breast pump has said to me, always in all stresses:

Right now
Let's go
You're a star!
Real quick
Shut up
Let it go
Not now
Let go
O.K.

5.

If my breasts were a building by Frank Lloyd Wright, following Wright's manifesto:

An honest ego in a healthy body
An eye to see nature
A heart to feel nature
Courage to follow nature
The sense of proportion (humor)
Appreciation of work as idea and idea as work
Fertility of imagination
Capacity for faith and rebellion
Disregard for commonplace (inorganic) elegance
Instinctive cooperation

then the nursing couple is above all this: this uncommon elegance, instinctive cooperation, idea as work, work as idea. My baby, a sapling, latched to the infrastructure of my leafy breasts, doubles her weight early, tugging at the next month. Then we are ready.

6.

A U.S. senator for the first time breastfeeds during a vote. It took a new law to allow this. In 2018: the first senator to give birth while in office. In Iceland, a senator drew international attention for the act, which she thought was ordinary life. Not trying to be an icon: "You've got to do what you got to do."

7.

There are Native women in Alaska who are afraid to nurse: there are toxins in the water, the air, the fish. Taking the land is taking everything, even sometimes the peace to nurse your baby. Yet women are resilient or they need to be.

*8.*

I wanted to put up a flyer for a breastfeeding support group, but Resident Services said the rendering of a nursing mother and her baby was "inappropriate." The baby devouring the breast, nothing visible but hunger.

Places I've pumped:

Amtrak bathroom
Bathroom at the Holocaust Museum in tears having seen images of women with their babies in line for the showers
Behind a divider in the nurse's office at school
My car while driving
The trunk of my car at a state park
Not in a glass office
At a drag show
Where a woman beside me was building a puppet stage
In a room with other women doing the same thing
While sorting bras, tampons, and maxi pads for women who are homeless

Places I've breastfed:

The dentist's while they were working on my mouth
In the grass
In a bathroom
In the dark in the New Orleans heat when the power went out
In a meeting
On the beach
At the mall in a corner facing the wall
In the heart of a tree which fell into a bench
In the blueberry orchard
Pretty much everywhere
While making eggs; while reading a story to my other children; while talking on the phone; while grocery shopping; while reading.

*9.*

Allen Ginsberg cried out to his mother, Naomi, who had just died: "O glorious muse that bore me from the womb, gave suck first mystic life & taught me talk and music."

*10.*

My son, red dye from his snow cone all over his face, says, "Take a picture, Mommy, while I'm happy." My baby's neck is always collecting droplets of milk, of fuzz, happiness slushing around.

# "Imaginary Gardens with Real Toads"

All artists give you back the suck of forbidden fruit.
Victoria DeBlassie making artwork out of hundreds of oranges,
dried down to brown-gold peels hooked together
into a sculptural fabric to give you back the suck
and scent of an orange. She convinces the train-station stand
in Florence to give her the vestiges of
oranges after they're pressed,
ripped, flipped inside out, juiced—
the bed-of-little-carrots pulp popped
like bubble wrap. In San Francisco she takes rinds from restaurants
like a mother-skunk dipping her head in the garbage pail.
In Albuquerque, her yoga studio and her sisters
cast off rinds like T-shirts, with tank-tops underneath.
From her own and everyone else's breakfast,
she collects the shells to craft *A Smell Wall*; *Accumulated Matter*;
*Interior Walls*; a pair of leather pants; and a whole igloo.

In a breastfeeding class, they told me sucking
and tearing at the rind, bending it back as you tore
the flesh in your mouth, suctioning,
bursting the pulp, this was suckling,
whereas bottle-feeding was plopping
a straw into an orange slice to draw up one drop.
My great-grandmother sent navel oranges by train to my father
from her groves. Every year after she passed, her children
mail-ordered oranges at Christmas. When I named my daughter
after my great-grandmother, that was the winter I started buying the oranges
big as grapefruit. I could see how Freud and Breuer's Anna O.
lived off oranges and drank no water,
just the splashes of juice dripping from the rows of pulp,
and the back of her hand rubbing it off her cheek. Anna O. dreaming
in and out of her "hysterical" life, perfumed in her reminiscences in how many languages,
however many free associations, affects, talking cures, schools of thinking.

## Emily Dickinson Keeping House, 280 Main Street

Dickinson, is that you, brass-knuckling the dough—
you behind the mask of a half-open cabinet door, white
apron stuffed with scraps, envelopes, and bleeding pen?
Licking the tips of the scarlet thread for your stack,

which would be flung open after your funeral in the library?
So "safe in their alabaster chambers," your echoey, dialectical souls
dreaming, folded up in drawers and chests
your brother's lovers fight over,

and there is always your sister L. looking.
Did you really report to the IRS your occupation is keeping house?
Skimming milk, massaging bouncy flour into flickering
yeast, you fall into the handwritten dark

of "the soul overhearing itself."
Domestic poems on wrappers, scraps, "gorgeous nothings,"
envelopes, out of slivers of light between chores.
The heat of it all while the bread rises the second time, longer.

Sometimes writing not by window but misty pillow.
Not that you are ever alone. You have your poems, letters, all the no ones,
"the hills, the sundown, a dog large as [yourself], the noise in the pool
excelling [your] piano, brother, sister, a mother who doesn't care for

Thought, a father too busy with his briefs to notice."
The you I know is by schoolgirl heart. Tell me,
not now, but not never, what rose in you like beads of yeast.
My daughter knows it's a new day though her hands look the same.

Whenever, in your poems, "shatter me with dawn."

## On Seeing a Lock of Plath's Hair

In the city, streetlights threw out darkness
like the hardest plum you'd ever felt,
but fake light didn't know anything
about how darkness was supposed to feel.

The night wakes the moon,
giving unseen thoughts a tongue
because only moonlight can really
divide comings and goings from nightly

quietude. Because night is *look,*
*you're driving across the country*
*and talking to someone you love*
*without being looked at.*

I'm losing darkness except in the wilderness
where a nocturnal sky is thumbed and dog-eared
by little fantastic stars.
Except the real, dark dreams

your soul finds while the body practices
dying. Except the dreamer's Bic pen tilting
lyrics inside a shoebox lid to
silence the numbing florescence of warehouses.

Darkness never forbids
a little natural light, as in Sylvia Plath's childhood
ponytail, culled in a museum,
cut by a mother after twelve years of

ash-blonde flipping. Girlhood wanes
and waxes blithely. Plath switched hair from
auburn to platinum blonde and back again.
Nightfall lets her—it's okay, *Write it!*—pulse

her typewriter keys like hooves over the river. She goes off.

# 2.

# Cento on Hysteria

O Sylvia, Sylvia // the death we said we both outgrew / the one we wore on our skinny breasts.[1]
I saw the best minds of my generation destroyed by madness, starving hysterical naked.[2]
The apt and curious *talking cure* and the humorous *chimney-sweeping* . . . it was necessary to resort to chloral.[3]
Hysteria is not a pathological phenomenon and can in every respect be considered a supreme vehicle of expression.[4]
Expos[ing] the slips, dreams, and jokes of individuals paraded as normal.[5]
I had hysterical impulses, with tears and convulsions. I had no resource except reading.[6]
I wanted to dictate my own thrilling letters.[7]
No one has had a proper idea of the complications of the psychical processes at work in hysteria, the juxtaposition of the most diverse impulses, the reciprocal connection of opposites, instances of repression and displacement and so on . . .[8]
The degree to which the *bad self*, as she herself called it, influenced her.[9]
After all, leaving women sitting around in empty houses had been the specialty of all

1. Anne Sexton, "Sylvia's Death" (1963), in *The Complete Poems of Anne Sexton* (New York: Houghton Mifflin, 1999), 126.
2. Allen Ginsberg, "Howl" (1955–56), *Collected Poems, 1947–1997* (New York: Harper Perennial, 2006), 134.
3. "Fräulein Anna O. (Breuer)" (1892), in Sigmund Freud and Josef Breuer, *Studies in Hysteria*, trans. Nicola Luckhurst (New York: Penguin, 2004), 34.
4. André Breton and Louis Aragon, "First Manifesto of Surrealism" (1925), in Elisabeth Roudinesco, *Jacques Lacan & Co.: A History of Psychoanalysis in France, 1925–1985*, trans. Jeffrey Melhman (Chicago: University of Chicago Press, 1990), 7.
5. "Femininity and Its Discontents" (2005), in *The Jacqueline Rose Reader* (Durham, N.C.: Duke University Press, 2011), 42.
6. Fyodor Dostoevsky, "Notes from Underground" (1864), in *White Nights and Other Stories*, trans. Constance Garnett (New York: Macmillan, 1923), 86.
7. Sylvia Plath, *The Bell Jar* (New York: Bantam Books, 1971; rpt., 1981), 62.
8. Sigmund Freud, "Fragment of an Analysis of Hysteria (Dora)" (1905), in *The Penguin Freud Reader* (New York: Penguin, 2006), 532.
9. "Fräulein Anna O. (Breuer)," 49.

men for ages. And for ages, when the men arrived, women bestirred themselves to cook supper—luckily, it was not yet common knowledge that many a woman had narrowly avoided committing murder by calmly breaking a few eggs.[10]

The art of daydreaming. Her private theater.[11]

One reads poetry with one's nerves.[12]

Suck, little babe, Oh suck again! / It cools my blood; it cools my brain.[13]

Which gives us the strongest sense of the force of the unconscious as a concept against a fully social classification relying on empirical evidence.[14]

The greatest poetic discovery of the latter part of the century.[15]

Coughing, shaking. Loss of voice. Not understanding when several people speak at once. Twenty-seven times. Becoming deaf during a deep absence. Twelve times.[16]

What image of poetic endeavor is now most universally despised? The consumptive man in his garret? The dilettante heiress who supports other writers? The hermit spinster? The prosperous professional who writes on the side? The woman with three names who muses piously on love, bowers, and the deaths of mothers and babies? That's clearly it. Yes, the poetess, the sentimental one.[17]

And you came each / weekend. But I lie. / You seldom came. I just pretended / you, small piglet, butterfly / girl with jelly bean cheeks, / disobedient three, my splendid // stranger. And I had to learn / why I would rather / die than love . . .[18]

Crazed through much child-bearing / The moon is staggering in the sky.[19]

10. James Baldwin, "Come Out the Wilderness," in *Going to Meet the Man: Stories* (1965; rpt., New York: Vintage, 1995), 221

11. "Fräulein Anna O. (Breuer)," 26.

12. Wallace Stevens, "Adagia" (1934–1940?), in *Opus Posthumous: Poems, Plays, Prose* (New York: Vintage, 1989), 189.

13. "The Mad Mother" (Wordsworth, 1798), in William Wordsworth and Samuel Coleridge, *Lyrical Ballads, 1798 and 1802* (Oxford: Oxford University Press, 2013), 64.

14. Rose, "Femininity and Its Discontents," 42.

15. Breton and Aragon, "First Manifesto of Surrealism," 6.

16. "Fräulein Anna O. (Breuer)," 40; Freud, "Fragment of an Analysis of Hysteria (Dora)," 461.

17. Annie Finch, "Confessions of a Postmodern Poetess" (1999), in *The Body of Poetry: Essays on Women, Form, and the Poetic Self* (Ann Arbor: University of Michigan Press, 2008), 120.

18. "Double Image" (1960), in *The Complete Poems of Anne Sexton*, 39–40.

19. "The Crazed Moon" (1933), in *The Collected Poems of W. B. Yeats* (London: Wordsworth Editions, 2000), 205.

What does a woman want?[20]

Why are women so much more interesting to men than men are to women?[21]

What this meant for the hysterical woman is that instead of just being looked at or examined, she was allowed to *speak*.[22]

(The body speaking because there is something which cannot be said.)[23]

I have found something worse / to meditate on.[24]

And, in after years, / When these wild ecstasies shall be matured / Into a sober pleasure; when thy mind/ Shall be a mansion for all lovely forms.[25]

I kissed a stone / I lay stretched out in the dirt / And I cried tears down.[26]

That crazed girl improvising her music / . . . Her soul in division from itself.[27]

The girl changed to bird and found a kind of rest. / Her new small brain gave her own sorrows no room. . . . After they've killed me, don't forget what I've said.[28]

She stood in desperate music wound, / Wound, wound, and she made / . . . no intelligible sound / But sang . . .[29]

I verily believe she thinks it is the writing which made me sick! But I can write when she is out, and see her a long way off from these windows.[30]

All day she plays at chess with the bones of the world.[31]

For all good poetry is the spontaneous overflow of powerful feelings: and though this be true, Poems to which any value can be attached were never produced on any variety of subjects but by a man who, being possessed of more than usual organic sensibility, had also thought long and deeply.[32]

20. Sigmund Freud, letter to Princess Marie Bonaparte (1925), qtd. in Ernest Jones, *Life and Work of Sigmund Freud*, vol. 2 (New York: Basic Books, 1953), 421.
21. Virginia Woolf, *A Room of One's Own* (New York: Houghton Mifflin, 1925; rpt. 1981), 27–28.
22. Rose, "Femininity and Its Discontents," 43.
23. Rose, "Femininity and Its Discontents," 43.
24. Yeats, "Crazy Jane on the Mountain" (1936–39), *The Collected Poems*, 295.
25. William Wordsworth, "Lines Written a Few Miles above Tintern Abbey" (1798), in *Lyrical Ballads*, 90.
26. Yeats, "Crazy Jane on the Mountain," 295.
27. Yeats, "A Crazed Girl," 259.
28. Cassandra in Aeschylus's *Agamemnon* (c. 458 BC), trans. Timothy Chappell, the Open University, 2013, http://www.open.ac.uk/people/sites/www.open.ac.uk.people/files/files/aeschylus-agamemnon-definitive.pdf, lines 1145, 1146, and 1317.
29. Yeats, "A Crazed Girl," 259.
30. Charlotte Perkins Gilman, "The Yellow Wall-Paper" (1892), in *The Yellow Wall-Paper, Herland, and Selected Writings* (New York: Penguin, 2019), 184.
31. Plath, "Female Author" (juvenilia), in *The Collected Poems of Sylvia Plath* (New York: Harper Perennial, 1981), 301.
32. Wordsworth, "Preface to *Lyrical Ballads*" (1802), in *Lyrical Ballads*, 98.

Only her tight, tight eyes were left. They were always left. . . . They were everything. Everything was there, in them. . . . She would see only what there was to see: the eyes of other people.[33]

Even her waking dreams we used—to silence our own nightmares.[34]

A fire was once within my brain.[35]

Peel off the napkin, / O my enemy / Do I terrify?——[36]

33. Toni Morrison, *The Bluest Eye* (1970; repr., New York: Penguin, 1993), 45, 47.

34. Morrison, *The Bluest Eye*, 205.

35. Wordsworth, "The Mad Mother," in *Lyrical Ballads*, 63.

36. Plath, "Lady Lazarus" (1960), in *The Collected Poems*, 244.

# Disruptions to the Sonnet by the Senior Class of 2000

We were analyzing that sonnet by Edna St. Vincent Millay
when someone in our class pierced his eyebrow with a safety pin,
and that was the end of his senior year. His proud, sad
head, those too-long eyelashes, trapped in that desk the color of
gray snow residue on the noses of cars. While some laughed,
others said "self-harm," a new word in the mouth.
What is the difference, really, between self-mocking
and self-effacing? a multiple-choice question could beg you into worrying.
We were so busy protesting his expulsion with a month left until graduation.
And all that praying, which could rally only the heart, only your own. We were
    busy crying, in
plum and red kilts, that he should just be able to walk, when, wait,
there was a girl who'd buried her father and she could smell him in some of the
    boys' faces as their
Old Spice deodorant reproved death and brought a man to life
in the aegis of their armpits, the holy scent even on their chins.

I tucked my head into a notebook, my back against my bedroom door that didn't lock,
then rushed into my older brother's room with my new poem.
He made all my words crooked: "Better I rip it up right now
than your teacher!" But how he missed novels I read, which we couldn't discuss
while he recovered, but thank God his suicide attempts were all like unformed deaths
    inside me.
I should say *inside him*, but it wouldn't feel true.
We pondered everything on the orange couch, brother and sister,
I'd only an hour before analyzed in the circle with the whole class,
and once it was Millay wary of love, though we were too young to be wary of love, still
a part of some songs and so many summers. The first concert I went to,
the beautiful David Banner knocked me over, in the caesura of his line,
as he flew from the stage to the balcony, and I thought, *This is living.*
*This is art.* My pangs that followed, trying to work out
what it meant, and why. Like "the rain is full of ghosts tonight."

# Excavated from an Unmarked Grave

B78, a Medieval Nun with Expensive Taste in Ink

Shaping paintbrush tips
in her mouth, she speckled
her tartar with blue

ink unknowingly
to illustrate texts like eyes
of pharaohs gilded

ultramarine. The
benign vanity of a
female scribe.

Can an artist whose
skeletal mouth told all die?
Say less than her own

library burnt down?
The blue beneath those hundred-
eye feathered frills, the

color of the Psalms.
There she goes, sprouting indi-
go all over us

like the Madonna's
robe pooling our winged
longing. Neon blue

sirens in the tide,
sunned deep lowering you in.
An art thief pulled in-

side brushstrokes of deep
blue on a museum wall,
plucked what lifted him:

incanting Rimbaud
to the moon, scaling the
building like a spi-

der, tingling with a
new system of nerves.
Her heart on a blue-lined note
a girl hid in her mouth: she had to.

## To Nicholas Hawksmoor, Architect of a Baroque Nervous System of Churches

Nicholas, what a past you are, a crypt doorway
at St Alfege, the sex in St Anne's bell
tower, shoes this girl buys in Stepney
to say she's tough,

the East End where St George is, who is three
Georges, one insane who was saying *What? What? What?*
real fast, shaking hands with a bush he thought had been one
of the ambassadors.

The devil is important, also. Tell me how we're him,
when it's a surgeon and architect, Sir Christopher Wren's idea, the fire
so he can get commissioned to build new sights, nothing like
those pigeons burning

over our heads, still going for a V like they do until both
wings burnt off and the bird, it has no choice, Nicholas.
Wren put you where you are, making up churches for Anne
like out of nowhere,

so why should you feel unorthodox? A pyramid with glass
unicorns and lions, King George, pineapples, gigantic keystones,
is in your head, fine, draw them as steeples.
Not like our fathers cared

because everything is on its Philosophers' Stone, Mercury of Seven
Eagles, or Green Lion, half on methane waiting as luna, balsam
of sulfur, cinnabar, marcasites to go into a gold—all being
the same, you know this.

## Breakup Scenery

is worse the worse the transportation, the Peter Pan bus that's going to break
down on the Manhattan Bridge, and no one gets their money back.
Or is worse the better the view, the lingerie from him she was wearing, her satin red-

hearted crotch when he quit it where they began, in a dorm bunk bed, not enough sheet.
Something was definitely over among all that good weed everywhere but no silverware,
inside the Utz chip bag embracing tampon trash in the finale of period sex, in the broken

door Samsoned apart one coked-out night. On a rooftop deck he hadn't put the railing in,
the tallest man told his wandering wife, "I just can't get hard for a bitch." A young professional
could have died at those last words, "You're going down, I'm going up," as the elevator's red-

lit number three flared his circled inferiority to another man's groomed sixth-floor ego.
 It has always
been worse: the engagement that rubbed off in the shower, a favorite place to cry to ghosts.
Or, "I'm tired of being angry and alone"—so mutual, who said it out loud first? The break-

down in the cereal aisle when a woman said she'd bought a house in another state.
 Or the dude
who, losing his father to cancer, caressed his dad's dying wish that he should get his
 shit together
only by leaving premarital sex for pious wife material. Loving you—the inside of a tent,
 the tracks unreadable

across a moving train, a hand branching atop my knee—smack on a set almost ridiculing
 the heart-level.
After I lost my virginity came what I thought was the saddest breakup,
"You'll have to find someone else to fuck you," when everything, like love, was misread.

# As if Part Of

In the Magic Mirror Maze, the man with the bad leg
says to Rita Hayworth's reflections, "Killing you
is like killing me, Lover," in a complex
version of the classic American two-shot.

She's just a former geisha who didn't smoke at first,
dress in nothing like Lady Gaga,
or wear nothing but for chilled Chanel Chance
you could run to like food on the fridge shelf,

pure, wet, cold, flash of a life,
luxury in a bachelor fridge with nothing but takeout.
Hayworth, the scent of the close-up.
Diving off a cliff,

leaning at the wide wheel of a yacht,
kissing Welles in the aquarium
near passing squid
where schoolchildren like to be, up close,

fingers on the glass to drum-pet sea monsters through it.
How after the split in real life,
Hayworth and Welles, still filming,
still yelled to each other on the set

on the yacht, forgot to stop pet names, Mama
and Papa who helps her reach back into his jacket, strange
squid in her damp swimsuit, who convinces her to wear short hair,
coiffed in a solo you'd remember as signature.

# This Girl I Lost Touch With

This girl, who was afraid to enter a room—
this girl conceived in the woods, on moss,
whose family dreamt under quilts,
who wore dresses that matched
anything fabric in the house,
even the dresses without loneliness—

I held her hand in the corridor-dark until
the speaking-in-tongues at the community college
dispersed into prayers with too many gerunds
and too much fervor that wouldn't adjust
if you got a thousand dollars in the mail
or jury duty, faith subtle as a crucifix
the size of God on the highway.

I waited with her until it was over,
although the prayer group was never really over.
Over rooms of crowded faith-based humidity, she
loved corridors of woods, the rushes of running away.

This girl and I, we were cult-lured but then
the leader "stepped down"—was it porn, alcohol,
Vicodin? The first time I drove in a man's car, there weren't
doors. I was eighteen so I fell in love: looking straight ahead
together, arm hair touching, the cathedral of autumn
anticipating a shape to hold you, the wind
that you sometimes hollered over.
What happened I can't see, but when he left
the group, I left: the death of visions.

This girl longed for someone too in her fingernails,
and without talking, just takes a man from his pregnant
wife's side, has his even newer children,
this girl who wouldn't go in a room all alone,
walked right in, somewhere we've not been, and never left.

## With Rosemary

There was a time when everything of hers
was tossed or given to any family member: the shelf dust of
Shakespeare, blue dust of the Madonna, the plaster dust of
Cherokee faces as the mixed stardust someone called
us all, flakes off the cosmos. Gold is the plains, the food we eat,
the heart sometimes, the brazenness of the gun in the new-to-them
world, but gold is the baby-wearing back, with the baby sleeping.

My grandmother's got footage from the Holy Lands and
not the stolen lands except in the resonance of her
prayer-chants. I remember she slept naked, brushed her hair
naked in the morning. Her other name was Lover.
Of her strange embattled piety, her healings under different
utterances with different waters, what was belief when
there was only believing? The only time she rose to anger
was in the gong of a few clashing dishes in the sink, in the muttering
of how not-mad she was, and, if overtaken by sorrow, she made the smallest
rolls, her children could eat ten of them, each.
A child she lost like her mother buried a child is why she left her son's
last highlighted page open like a secret between them.

Nearly a century old, my grandmother, after surgery,
seated in her matrilineal silence before the raid of
thinking her thoughts, folded into herself, her spine a singular
wave of corn titled down, she just lifted the hem
of her shirt so carefully, scanning the shirt like a text,
the smooth flowery fabric she mumbled Shakespeare into,
"There's rosemary, that's for remembrance. Please remember, love."
Deep memory back after the knife, the stitch like a buried accent
slips out only when drinking, or very tired. Myths like the wide picture
books in the fabric of womanly adornment, storied blankets, coats
of lost mothers you could always remember direct from the lap,
wearing a part of the story on your frame: my grandmother
reading her shirt, what is she, reading, trying to remember?

# 3.

# The Matrix Miscellany

*Introductory Note*

For two months in the summer of 2017, I did archival research at the Folger Shakespeare Library in Washington, DC. I had proposed a project called "Author Comma a Lady" for a short-term fellowship. The project would study early modern poetry by so-called lady authors as well as the early modern practices of creating poetic miscellanies (anthologies) and composing cookbooks and receipt (recipe) books. I sensed a parallel between the work of constructing a poetry anthology and the labor of compiling domestic medicine and receipt books—many included the work of anonymous women. I received the fellowship and drafted about fifteen pages of poetry, but the imprint of my time would linger beyond the composition of these poems. I didn't expect to engage with the model of a poetic miscellany, of scattered verses and voices, but it seemed suggestive of my own hysterical intertexuality: my engagement with the past and my reaching for female literary models in whatever form I could find them in. It reminded me of how my own grandmother's creativity has been passed down to me in a diary and a cookbook, and of how Alice Walker would locate her mother's creativity in a garden and in quilts. The culmination of my study came in the form of a poetic miscellany I've called "The Matrix Miscellany," reflective of primeval concerns around the womb or "matrix" (an early modern term), and of the myriad ways women have pieced together knowledge about their bodies and turned to each other and to matrilineal sources of domestic medicine and folklore. At the same time, women themselves have been pieced together by male-dominated medicine, silenced by male-dominated narrative medicine, and violated with cold forceps and precepts that have long sought to name, know, and control women. Male practitioners have attempted to cure aspects of their own incongruous, jagged emotional lives by projecting them and locating them in the "hysterical" female body.

During my fellowship, I expected to discover poems by anonymous lady authors in early modern poetic miscellanies, and I thought that they might be fodder for my own poetry and poetry criticism. I soon found myself terribly bored by homages to random flowers as in O GREAT BLACK-EYED SUSAN! My students would call this flowery flower poetry "cringey," and, similarly, I felt embarrassed to be in the presence of such sentimental, provincial drivel, as if I could make any kind of connection to an homage that beheld, in the narrator's haze of self-effacing wonder, a common flower (and without irony or complex narrative threads). I thought immediately of Alicia Ostriker's "What Do Women (Poets) Want?: Marianne Moore and H.D. as Poetic Ancestresses," and of the conflicted feelings contemporary women poets have about their poetic foremothers: "When a women says she cannot locate poetic mothers, I think it means something like the following. She too despises the mob of scribbling women and wants to dissociate from their presumed mediocrity. . . . If a woman is ambitious and means perhaps to be a major poet . . . she will not, in connection with women poets, have often encountered terms like great, powerful, forceful, violent, brilliant, or large" (2). I think for many women writers, the lineage of poetesses (a term Annie Finch embraces) is always tinged with discomfort. But, in pushing through that disassociation, I was happy to find in Aphra Behn something "great, powerful, forceful, violent, brilliant, [and] large"—as I did in works by many anonymous "lady authors." For example, a sampling of woman-authored elegies were occasioned by child-loss; sometimes a woman mourned the seventh infant she had to bury due to a stillborn birth, miscarriage, or sickness; metaphors of withered blossoms and longing maternal trees or branches felt confessional, personal, raw. I thought of a female friend who lost her newborn baby after just three days; her oldest child includes this baby (named) in family pictures, and even to write this is to cry for my friend. I thought of my husband's teenage student in New Orleans who brought a picture to school of her stillborn baby. There is still so much silence around infant loss, and no one asks, "Tell me about your baby." Many of the early modern elegies for miscarried babies were even filled with self-disdain and self-blame, reflecting the early modern idea that miscarriages were somehow the fault of the woman, caused by lust, frigidity, bad thoughts, poor health, or even fear of miscarriage.

In reading anthologized medicinal remedies in various cookbooks, I discovered a kind of found poetry in women's quotidian, practical writing and archiving. I became immersed in the idea of writing as a form of female reproduction meant to manage the bodily uncertainties of female biological reproduction. In domestic remedies, the language of cure was a kind of inter-century connection and conversation between women about their bodies. I felt an uncanny sisterhood with the women behind the collective texts of receipt books—as if these texts were an alterative to twenty-first-century blogs where members pose and answer questions about conception, lactation, child loss, the choice to reproduce, and postpartum depression. Instead of googling a question such as "Am I making enough milk?" and then stumbling upon KellyMom.com, where I end up reading something affirming that makes me trust my body to produce enough milk for my baby, I was turning to early modern remedies through which women of another time were passing on knowledge and care to each other. This incredible body of work written by women combats the absurdities of the male-authored diagnoses of "hysteria," which seemed to be a catch-all diagnosis for any ailment a woman suffered from. The symptoms of hysteria overlap with various current diagnoses such as anxiety, depression, bipolar disorder, mania, postpartum depression, schizophrenia, fever, the plague, a cough, the common cold, shortness of breath, obsessive-compulsive disorder, or borderline personality disorder. In early modern England, as in other historical times and even today, women are often shamed, not listened to, and then told what is happening in their own bodies. So voiceless were the emotional lives of "hysterical" women that it comes as a sign of progress when Freud listens to Dora, and records some of her speech. What if in telling Freud that this is the last therapy session, Dora was dismissing not the process of the "talking cure" (a term a female patient of Freud's coined) but the power dynamic itself?

In doing this research, I came to understand how early modern women were performing a kind of talking cure in conversing with each other in these medicinal books about their own reproductive rights, bodies, pain narratives. Is sharing an abortive medicine, for instance, a way in which women weren't waiting for legal permission? Buried within traditional early modern cookbooks were folkloric cures for all things female, which, in this context, meant all things reproductive. I found myself drawn to domestic medicine, particularly the cures for "fits of the mother," hysteria, low milk supply in lactating mothers, as well as abortive medicines, medicines for staying beautiful during the Plague, and cures for hysterical children, which I took to mean lively, robust, emotionally-in-touch children—in short, children like my own. I spent my time hunting down more and more medicinal receipt books, and I discovered a particularly lovely index of "women's" reproductive health issues at the back of one volume. I noticed a similarity between a medicinal recipe for lactation and the ingredients of Mother's Milk tea, which a female friend had given me; I also noticed that the nursing beers of today are similar to those of the early modern era.

As I read through the litany of alternative medicines for "hysteric fits of the mother" and "ease in labor," I dreamed back through my own emergency C-section and the finite baby blues that followed the birth of my first child,

Juliet (they did not follow the birth of my second or third baby). In my study, it became evident to me that across time, the birthing mother is often not in control of her body, her birth, or her medical narrative. I gave birth not long after the documentary *The Business of Being Born* (2008) was gaining traction; socially, I felt judged by my friends who were able to live out their natural birth plans, and I felt like a failure, as though my body had failed me, when I underwent an emergency C-section for my first child, and, later, had two repeat C-sections for my next two children. After interrogating me as to why I had C-sections, friends would even point out that I could have had VBACs since I had been robbed before—as though to compensate for the first birth experience. I remember a man bragging to me about how his wife just had to prove she could do it, and so she had three C-sections and one VBAC, though for the latter she had to travel to find the one doctor who would take her. How proud he was that she did it. Even John Berryman yelps through the textual body of Anne Bradstreet, "I did it with my own body," and I feel threatened. Among my own friends (or even strangers at the park) who glowed about their natural births and congratulated each other for "completing" after thirty- or sixty-hour labors, I felt like a pariah for having had a C-section (which would, in my case, necessitate C-sections for my other two children). In many conversations, I have not even felt comfortable sharing my first birth narrative since I have been criticized and interrogated by friends and some relatives despite the emergency nature of my situation. The essentialist narrative of natural birth is about empowerment for some but disembodiment, fragmentation, and vulnerability for me, and I suspect for others. However, I went on to feel a great sense of pride, bodily autonomy, and sisterhood with other lactating moms, and have found breastfeeding to be an essential part of my motherhood experience. The maternal body is both a site of belonging and a site of alienation; and even the mother-nursling dyad, an emblem and source of immense belonging, can be called into question or, worse, shunned or shamed by others in a public space.

I could easily imagine early modern mothers consulting cures in domestic medical receipt books, and feeling the vissimilitudes of connection and dissonance. Somehow, this excited me greatly like the first time I took my baby (Juliet) to an art museum (the NOLA Museum of Art), and I saw a bronze sculpture of a nude mother and her koala-esque baby at her breast: *We're art!* I felt, looking at my baby begin to respond to art in her own way—staring at the light of a crystal art object, lunging in my arms towards a massive wooden boat, or smearing her fingers across a glass window that was filled with samovars (which I always wondered, in reading Chekhov, what they might look like).

While in residence at the Folger, I was bridging my own experiences not just with the rare manuscripts but with a community of scholars who were living what one of us called "just following your bliss." I recall a Folger blogger challenging her following to transcribe an early modern recipe and then to make it! At the Folger, during the daily afternoon tea in the basement, where scholars gathered to share ideas, pose questions, and ramble about their work, I found a kind of community of give-and-take not unlike the recipe anthologies and the poetic miscellanies I was reading upstairs, in the dim lighting, with foam wedges holding the book like an early modern car seat for the unwieldy, bulky texts I didn't want to break, wrinkle, or disrespect.

On the metro rides home from the Folger, I was writing, in a journal, my own poem about my mother's botched C-section and the trauma that resulted from it; what some might call hysteria was in cases such as hers actually PTSD. The only way to approach this subject matter, in my mind, was by merging the confessional with the archival. In the title poem of this book, "Hysterical Water," I brought together the early modern archival research with the inherited narrative of my mother's birth story (when she had my youngest brother). Using the cookbooks as a touchstone, as well as the male midwifery tradition, I grounded my mother's story and my own perspective in the cures related to women's reproduction—from fertility cures to postpartum care to "hysteria" treatments. The poem switches from excerpted and altered cures with their simple ingredients to the trauma narrative of my mother's experience. This was a formative story not only for my mother but for my family, and yet I had never been able to write it until I was riding the metro back from the Folger and jotting down thoughts in a journal about what cures across centuries can and cannot tell us, can and cannot do for us—and similarly, all that poetry, with its palliative, cathartic aims, can and cannot do. This poem, which I called "Hysterical Water," is my attempt to empathize with and understand my mother's traumatic birthing experience, for which there is no cure, or even language. I choose not to include "Hysterical Water" in this series, because the poem is ultimately a family history and felt like it should be the book's final piece.

The long poem that follows, "The Matrix Miscellany," is broken into seven sections; all of it comes from my stint at the Folger and scatters into the air little slips of paper with strange call numbers of rare books and an enormous desk with red pencils, notebook, laptop, and faded, scarlet books for peering into at a thirty-degree angle: I was too excited to sit, but stood. My models in writing this poem were the esteemed female writers who had spent time with the rare materials at the Folger as part of a 2012 *Shakespeare's Sisters* exhibit; among these works were Elisabeth Nunez's nonfiction essay about her grandmother's literary salon in Trinidad (an essay that formed the basis of a memoir, *Not for Everyday Use*), Maxine Kumin's poem "Sonnet Uncorseted," and Jane Smiley's lyric essay/story "Marguerite, Queen of Navarre, Gives Desdemona Advice." Though I never saw the exhibit, because I was living in New Orleans when it took place, I kept the exhibit publications with me in a black folder at all times, as a guide. I regularly forgot the locker code I'd set, or lost the slip of paper where I wrote it down, or couldn't figure out the directions and number of whirls on the dial, so there were my umbrella and wallet effacing me in a silence I never could figure out, in the dark matrix of a locker cell. Getting out of the library was harder than getting in—like the baby was easier going in than out. So many texts, codes, recipes to mystify and haunt me with their "Hey, we're really *s*'s but we look like *f*'s," early modern something.

### 1. *The Begetting Virtues according to a Man*

Though women be unlearned
(for the most part), and know only
those languages natural
to them, I am indebted to many matrons

and midwives
who have helped me write
*The Expert Midwife*
as a man.

All my labors
I bequeath to all grave,
modest and discreet women—
not for idle serving-men, profane fiddlers.

In volumes I could tell you of satyr births,
of how and with what instruments
dead children sticking
in the womb are to be brought forth.

Of certain Forceps.
Of the ordering of the woman
in childbed
and of the Infant being newly born.

Of witches and harlots who open the veins in the feet
of a pregnant woman who wants to get rid of It—
how they wash the woman's legs morning
and night in the vapor of wine.

Of a monster born of a woman,
no arms, a crooked foot with talons like a ravenous bird,
an eye on his knee, and in the midst of his breast he had
the Figure of a Cross.

What brings forth unripe fruit like
sudden fury, great danger, exceedingly great
fear, overmuch sorrow, sudden joy, desire
of things not to be gotten?

Too much seed or not enough,
lasciviousness in too much moisture of the Matrix
can a formless Feature make:
even four legs, two heads, and a tail.

Overmuch heat strangles
him in the womb. What could possibly annoy
the Feature worse than the noisome stinks and fumes of
lamps and candles newly put out?

Many also say the veins
placed behind the ears, which give way to the spirits,
which the brain communicates and imparts
to the seed, meddle with engendering.

Even as sprigs gather more
from the earth than from the plant, so infants
take from their mothers.
The mother must be comforted

in childbed. Take a conserve of roses,
tansy wormwood, cloves, a dram of violets
and marshmallow roots gathered fresh in a shepherd's
purse, a handful of strained raisins, and with
the syrup of rose, make an electuary, and let it be
gilded with a leaf of pure gold. Take it to the lips,
the gums, the tongue and underneath the tongue.
For when there is pain, for
when there is going to be pain.

*2. Authoress Contemplating Her Uterus*

The souls you think you quickened
early, souls which you talked to like God,
went ahead somewhere without you,
made you the child turned around
in the woods. You did what they said:
you never attended the funeral
of a child while pregnant.
You never rode in a carriage. You didn't fall
over roots even in your bed-rest dreaming.
You drenched your secret places in
soap made of hog's lard and damask roses.
You drank only lemon water.
You should have been as swift as an oiled
feather dancing across the porcelain cup
so the almonds don't stick to the inside.

When a letter miscarries,
it's not that it doesn't arrive at all,
but that it shows itself at a door where
the occupant's so bored he will knife
apart someone else's mail, the way
some trifling pedants will "do a book," "have done
that author," "love doing Shakespeare,"
"love doing it," "taught it six times."

The jaundiced face of a baby
the size of a muskmelon, wrinkled
and gilded, is an unheard narrative—
worse than a single loose sheet
falling out of the bottom of a clasped
poetic miscellany. The body loses whole
fragments like books in a fire, in water.

Leave it to the realms of the anonymous
to cast her words about the strange temples
with stalactites where the world begins,
cast her contemplations into the deep
hold of woman coteries concocting recipes
and poems, superstition and hymnal piety,
some with their ghosted interlocutors.

"With the blossom, blast the tree!"
Your prayer isn't for everyone to hear.
Know this: your baby wants you back too,
wants back the cordial of your womb-water,
duplicated in the smell of your colostrum.
Inside you, she must have worshipped
the whooshing of bloodflow in your
veins. Liked rearranging the items in the dark
purse of you to better flutter and catapult herself,
leaving you so little room to breathe.
You raise your arms as bendy Juniper branches
above your head, authoring more space where
there's none left. Stretching out, you two
conjure a new friendship within an existing one.
Do you know if her drumming, from inside a muffled
snare, was sharpest the moment you lay down for the night?
Isn't everyone happier like this, isn't that
the point? Your small hips try sending out
into the world, again, your life's life, and you don't want
to lose, but find your balance with your center of gravity
pulsing apart faster. You want to breathe in the
newborn smell, and put it into words, but it
welcomes you first before you know
a thousand ways a scent can make you cry.

### 3. *"The Thought of High Windows, and beyond It"*

Before a drone could hand-deliver the abortion pill to Irish girls. Before a doctor told Gloria Fucking Steinem, "First, you will not tell anyone my name. Second, you will do what you want with your life." Before the price of Plan B was twenty-three pounds, or before two doctors were needed to sign off for it. Before a nurse taped a seaside poster to the ceiling tiles for the patient to look at during the ordeal in case she would keep her eyes open the whole time. Before my friend, who needed money to even buy the pregnancy test to begin with, who had the operation done for free in England, told me she just can't eat alone now on her dorm bed, eat the frozen dinner, after saying, "I went by myself there, though it makes no sense." But then, an early modern woman carried the baby a man shot up in her whole like a cavalier vessel, and she only had to detain it for so long a life as formed and definite as a brother's or sister's. She was a poor carriage, or good carriage, of whatever man engendered. An abortion meant something untimely: miscarriage, termination, stillborn, never-named. Then, women talked among themselves of ant pastes, wines, special baths, poisons, powders of rue, myrrh, pennyroyal, and myrtle. Then, the *W* index of cookbooks or "receipt books"—domestic medicine for women's complaints, all reproductive—echoed a coterie of women talk and women work, women grief. The ideas, an older sister you never had, an aunt who was young. Ideas for how to dry away the milk in your breast, how to increase your milk supply with wheat beers, how to solve fits in children, how to preserve your hair. How to stop endless menses. But not how to deal with life's shittiest verses, tormenting seductions, traumas of bittersweet, formless features. Just the paste of smeared berries, insects, flowers, and poisons, a vaginal cordial, here.

*4. If You Googled, in Another Century, the Female Complaint, No Quotes . . .*

SYMPTOMS

Dejection of mind, anxiety, difficulty breathing,
weeping, heart palpitations, et cetera.
Hysterical fits commence with pain,
a sense of fullness near the navel,
spreading towards the left side.
Like a ball passing upward,
sticking in the throat,
inciting the sense of suffocation

until the limbs are agitated,
the mind in a stupor,
and the body falls down.

SCENE

The woman, half-open mouth, wild feet,
arching of the back, suggestive of thrusts,
spasmodically laughing, crying, screaming,
sighing, sobbing like a deranged prophetess
reading the elegy on the wall.

This followed by soreness over the whole body,
then profound sleep.

CAUSES

Changes in the organs of generation.
Puberty, menstruation, pregnancy, labor,
and being delivered of child.
Caused by cold, intemperate climates.
Caused by over-moisture or dryness.

### A CASE STUDY

Hysterical affectations greatly afflict women in labor. Mother
of five: gloomy forebodings, low spirits, weeping and agitation,
in the Great Despair that comes with peculiar
sensitivity of the nervous system.

### TREATMENT

Tansy tea, nervine and antispasmodic tinctures,
laxative bitters, and the free use
of cayenne pepper.
Bathing of the breasts in oils
for one hour.
Pressed witch-hazel leaves for injections
in the vagina.

The patient should sit by the fire,
her feet in hot water,
collar bones, neck, shoulders, breasts covered with quilts
and cloak
to promote perspiration
and the inner workings
of the tinctures.

### IMPLICATIONS

The woman must not
be allowed to
despair.

Human consolation is
of little avail. It is rarely
the case that
any comfort
can be given.

### FOR FURTHER STUDY

We know where but not why.

### *5. Beauty in Time of Plague*

To survive plague through preservative remedies
by calling for the flesh of poisonous vipers,
the application of a pigeon, dead or live, by calling for your own
hot blood let out but never in summer,

calling for cinnamon toast or plain
buttered bread if you're poor, for the aloe of prayer;
calling for charms around your neck
is not the same as becoming more beautiful,

wanting to look in the mirror
when others are dying, when you know so are you.
All you need is someone
to lift your wet hair into a thread off your dewy neck.

Like a corpse waking to see another day, embalmed in turtle fat and Bordeaux.
Some say Keats robbed graves or didn't see why you wouldn't.
The poet unzippering the warmth in the earth clods
in so many bowery cathedrals of night.

Blazons zombify the world into
a teenage female corpse, hacked down to rows of strawberry nipples,
the towers of busty Lebanon, an upstream river between the legs,
a womb like flocks of everything on all fours, twin fawns, rose gardens.

When you made love the first time in the woods,
you didn't realize the tree had feelings that only Aphra Behn could satisfy,
singing the voyeuristic branches reaching for your breasts, the undone
corset, skeletal ribbon in the moss. Ménage à trois with a birch.

You want what you want, beauty in plague, vanity in
death. Middle-aged women of action making salve
from dog feces to soak raw sores in.
Escorting leeches. Fixing the Water of Life,

Cinnamon Water, Israel's Water, Water Good Against
Any Infection, Snail Water. But we go back to the baby
still pruning in amniotic fluid, scalp shaped by vaginal birth.
First love that comes before you know you are naked

or that you are so beautiful. Then, you are even to yourself
like unfrequented streets in a city whose customs
you don't know. My blonde-ish Indian-ish great-
grandmother's yellowed bridal gown,

leopard-printed in the back with
virginal blood, archival. Aired out like a specimen tingling
with wormwood, rue, vinegar, and rosewater correcting
the soggy air of old plague, oozing.

*6. Upon Hearing of the Shakespeare First Folio, Four Hundred Years Posthumous, Found in the Scottish Isle of Bute, I Think of My Father*

My father told me that once he knew the first audience believed in ghosts, it changed Shakespeare: everything made sense. In my father's heyday, college with its full cast of ghosts, the buildings named for the dead, the ancient dead studied and addressed, the pyramids a taunt, my father's only brother is brought out of basement-cold nothingness to be resurrected from the steps that seized then ejected him. You could say his ghost interferes with Option 2 on the Final: How does Shakespeare reinvent spirits so they are no longer mere machinery?

Your brother is now a phantom version of ourselves, an apparition so human that all his queasy messages require verification: this ghost's a looking glass that needs its own glass, a secret that still wants in on it.

Do the hands that held your brother together, momentarily, in the ambulance, after his last seizure, do they come back, come back wildly, to coax a thought open, to crack the cranium open like cauliflower florets, do your hands ever start to look like his hands?

My friend once told me that when she was looking at her uncle in the casket, she claimed it was her father and wept as if he was the dead. The first death comes reeling out of drawers in gothic mansions, a First Folio not aired in centuries, a loss, a new space where it left you so bright it hurts to look anyone in the eye after. Trembling wind that opens your eyes wider.

You said looking at him there in the casket, he'd lost his boyish look, as you, about to graduate, had lost yours—how you would fly eighteen miles each way to class on your yellow bike with the ram's horn handlebars, the plastic bag tied over the seat in weather, and the bungee-cord secured stack of plays on the back ledge—or else you hitchhiked to a college degree over highways, with your uncut hair, a cotton-candy bouffant-globe, no deodorant, and your hippy style of wearing Army jackets ironically. Perhaps your brother's look was the frozen boyhood of epilepsy he would never live to outlive, the eyes that say *Look after me, look after me. Who else will?* You said it was the first time, and so you almost didn't recognize the man looking at you.

*7. Floriography in Time of Silence*

I squashed droplets of garlic cloves inside one letter because I wanted him
to smell like the jerk he was bent on becoming. A declaration under his nails.

My handkerchief with the red roses invites a lover further like Ruth's hair
crossing the ankles of a man who will wake up at the threshold to more life.

The basic canary-yellow carnations replying to his hopeless yellow beacons are to say
I wanted a friend whose company was light in weather into more weather, but not in sunshine.

The stationery I made with this achingly red flora means I think about him more
than I should: look also, the plum tree from his country house where I stop breathing.

Where is baby's breath, a few carnations, a hieroglyphic twig, something for filler in my tone-
setting bouquet to slow-release my red dancing-tulip love? This one I can't suffocate.

White is the color of apologies, poppies the state of not being free. How can I say
in flowerspeak, I just don't know about us: "we know what we are, but not what we will be."

Pink is yes; sometimes Canterbury bluebells is a toneless acknowledgment.
Flowers don't mean the same thing when you consider the source, how hyperbolic,

genuine, or guarded the temperament of the couple. Remember Freud says
sometimes a cigar is just a cigar. All flowers act to liberate the heart

from monochromatic schema. Ophelia gives out flowers like last words—pansies for heart's
ease; rosemary for nostalgia; fennel for flattery; but the violets died with her nonstop father.

To herself, and the queen, almost a mother, rue for abortion, infidelity, disdain, even self-
loathing. In the sea-scrolls of her hair, a fantastic garland of all that couldn't ease her heart.

SELECTED WORKS CONSULTED AT THE FOLGER SHAKESPEARE LIBRARY IN PREPARATION FOR "THE MATRIX MISCELLANY"


Anonymous. "Address to a Sigh . . . by a Lady." In "Miscellaneous Collection in Prose and Verse" [manuscript, 1793–ca. 1800].

Anonymous [a lady author]. *An Essay in Defence of the Female Sex, in Which Are Inserted the Characters of a Peasant, a Quire, a Beau, a Vertuoso, a Poetaster, a City-critick, &c. in a Letter to a Lady.* London, 1696.

Bothwell, Lady Anne. "A Mother's Song to Her Son." In "Poetical Miscellany" [manuscript, ca. 1630].

Canning, Mrs. "Lines by . . . on Lord Erskine's Saying a Wife Was Like a Tin Canister Tied to a Dog's Tail." From "Miscellany Selected and Written by (Jane) Wilkinson and Her Friends" [manuscript, 1821–1842]. The North family collection of letters and papers relating to Tate Wilkinson, Mrs. Siddons, and the North family of York.

Carey, Mary. "Spiritual Dialogue, Meditations, and Poems" [manuscript, 1650–1658].

Carr, Anne. "Choyce Receits Collected out of the Book of Receits, of the Lady Vere Wilkinson" [manuscript, ca. 1674–1770].

"English Cookery and Medicine Book" [manuscript, ca. 1677–1711].

"Poetical Miscellany" [manuscript, late eighteenth century].

Rüff, Jakob (or James Reuff). *The Expert Midwife; or, An Excellent and Most Necessary Treatise of the Generation and Birth of Man, Wherein Is Contained Many Very Notable and Necessary Particulars Requisite to Be Knoyyne . . . Also the Causes, Signes, and Various Cures, of the Most Principall Maladies and Infirmities Incident to Women.* 6 vols. London, 1637.

Winchilsea, Anne Kingsmill Finch. *Miscellany Poems, on Several Occasions, Written by a Lady.* London, 1713.

Wright, Mrs. (Mehetable Wesley). "Address to Her Dying Infant" (Sept. 1728). In "Miscellaneous Collection in Prose and Verse in Which Are Included Several Original Pieces, 1793" [manuscript, 1793–ca. 1800].

Wroth, Lady Mary. "Pamphiilia to Amphilanthus: A Crown of Sonnets Dedicated to Love" [manuscript, ca. 1615–1620].

# 4.

## From a Woman Who Wants to Be Objectified in the Ways She Wants to Be

### 1. *How We Got Eyes*

When I talk to you in my head, Maestro, Canon, Word, God,
ask you to inhabit my editing voice so I can see if I have a poem,
I know I've gone too far. But so have you, Muse, haunting
early modern botanists who painted flora with the hairs of
squirrel tails fanning out of a quill,
dyes of tree gum, a poisonous, deep red
forged of mercury combustions,
or of smeared dead female insects for lighter shades.
Botanists mixing colors in mussels,
even painting six hours straight
in the fields, in the Heath because there were no touristy snapshots
with digital erasure, no one internet-famous. Better
yet to memorize a line than write it down,
the prayer in the cathedral that summed up
*Paradise Lost* in a fragment: "And though we were born into a holy world,
it is one that is tissued and structured with sin . . ."
I can't remember the rest, only that
we looked up—as if Evensong could botanize tourists—
made eye-contact at that moment.

### 2. *Adjectives for Everyone (like Beautiful)*

I stopped by your apartment for a letter of recommendation
and saw you even have an annotated scrapbook of clippings,
drawings, articles—which you call a commonplace book—on ginger. Why?
In Italy, a woman told us that all foreigners use the same three or four adjectives;
now you're adding to a small book you call *Adjectives for Everyone.*
What I want when you die? The belief that you told me, "Keats meant you
when he said 'beauty is truth.'" That it wasn't a line because no one ever
heard it, no students, wives, animals, specimens, inanimate objects you address
in the dark or write to, the pen strung to your towel rack in the powder room.

When will you finish the one that has Darwin's dog Piper,
Samuel Johnson's feline Hodge, and other pets of greats
in some delicious, existential conversation
we would feed upon, like orphans of Dickens-emaciation, on treacle syrup?

### 3. *Leaf in a Book*

And I want that leaf: I know you keep a specimen inside your folio
of *Paradise Lost,* a leaf so old that it makes you think it's from the goddamn tree
of good and evil; finding it again's easy. See the writing's in two ways, with four pages
to an open page. See the word *Notes,* one's upside down. An upside-down
word's not mirror image. It's not backwards either. What is it?
I know this much from breathing over the leaf:
you don't want to turn a specimen over—the envelopes are for particles
and seeds you lose. This plant isn't mounted,
but if it were, you'd want to keep it in a natural position. Something
in me wants in on the cleaving leaf, retrogressing to the deep calling for
more of itself, leaves over Eve and Adam's pelvises.
Nothing around Eve's upturned nipples but intimation.

### 4. *Neglected Young Woman with One Nice Pair of Underwear*

Pressed in a journal in the desk drawer—I know where—is a drawing of Sydney,
a she-seal from Australia, lying on an ice island for sun and air, chin lifted
like some seal-mermaid mutant a lost seaman invents as muse.
I don't know why I feel for her, Syndey, also where she's from,
but I'd like to bask like that, not needing a Bathsheba sob story either.
I dreamed I was Scarlett Johansson in Reeboks in a dorm room, ready to
rise in sci-fi super-hero fashion as the new gentlewoman princess
who tells men, even her husband, to "get over it"—
not caring one iota about what anyone has to say about the different selves
of a modern Renaissance woman.
I am ready to rise like her into indifference,
and shape-shift into the vocalist in a duet for a break-up album;
an operating-system voice and consciousness; photographer-poet;

a neglected young woman with one nice pair of underwear;
black widow; a ropey yoga teacher seeking cover in the office closet while her lover
satisfies his wife who also surprised him at work, on his desk; strong swimmer
affecting drowning; naive American journalist abroad; cropped, platinum blonde hair
on stage at the women's protest, with all those "I'm a Nasty Woman!" shirts, pink knit
pussy hats slanting up at her; or merciless warrior-assassin.

### 5. *The Queen of America Goes to Washington City*

Straying to a conference where I learn from a woman,
as if seeing for the first time,
Professor Berlant, whose ringlets shook as she wrung
out cinematic texts exploding with other, more callow brunette spirals
ramming into Parisian hotel curtains
the new vertical bed half a man is in, only half, and that half is an old Brando,
but Berlant, before the half O of bleachers at her talk,
she just blurts out, "It's not that feminists don't want to be
objectified, but that we all want to be objectified in the ways we want to be objectified."
Someone—the male participant who always talks first—said the theatrical sex
in *Last Tango in Paris* was rather self-admiring.
A woman said at least she could tell they were trying, that she likes it
when someone tries as Berlant nods a laugh, "Yes,
these are the conversations we are going to be having
at a Twenty-First Century Intimacy Conference," and you could feel her paper's favorite
footnotes jumping deeper down the page, scattering into shivering creeks
she'll erupt with floating trees, a few petals more loud than soft, some slit with wildlife.
It was possible, then, to have more than one nice pair of black lace underwear—and not to say
you wore them for yourself, because you didn't, as it was possible to flaunt them unto
objectification, if that was what one wanted, which I did,
and now if I wanted to sleep, my therapist said to put away the Lacan, the gender shit, the poetry,
the heady self-sabotaging wrecking balls of humanistic inquiry, but he was wrong about that.
After reading just those very things, I dreamt Berlant telling me to go for it.
An older woman at the conference said
she walked out after the butter scene, you know, the rape scene,
without the satisfaction of watching the chick kill the militant dullard, Brando,
while he's wearing her father's uniform, saying to the police

that she doesn't know his name—she never knew the guy. This is when Berlant,
hair random and wild, confesses she walked out of the theater then too
because that is what you did . . . and then taught the film later, writing her famous book,
of which there are several and they converse with you all at once, and you see, in a line
that has "the look of being looked at" the way those words want, that it's finally,
after all this, okay to want to be wanted if you want it.

## Recipe from My Grandmother for Self-Charity

After I'd singe my face a little, I'd wash my hair with the ashes.
The lesson is in the hurt of erasure. Because
my first love signed his name "With Oceans
of Love," but never knew I was pregnant with a son, only the

firstborn, a girl, before he died as one of those war heroes
mothers and wives never really let die. Because my first love signed
over his checks to me, and my second blessed me with the nickname
"Stupid," I had ways of talking myself out of great personal loss.

A whole year went by during which I never prayed one single day.
In the breathlessness or the excruciating sunkenness, the brain
dizzy as the stupefying heart, of summer afternoons longer than
years, I would remind myself I was once the May Queen, 109 pounds,

and I was the song, "Five-Foot-Two, Eyes of Blue." I was beautiful and I could
still have an ice cream. Everyone knew I loved your mother most
because I needed her. She'd watch the other five in the basement,
the walls with all your uncle's drawings of rats.

On bad days, I locked them out of the house. And those rats,
they must have brought with them the plague of sorrow.
You can only listen to so much trouble at once, preserving
better days in small glass bottles so you can have the best tastes

anytime you want from all seasons but winter. Winter's
for remembrance only, like those love letters I kept from the war and
said you can't take from the house even to copy. If anything
were to happen, when that's all I have of my real love. Widowed

twice, I'm ashamed to say I couldn't remember who
I was burying, Jim or Warren. I get so confused.
Did you know I have no teeth now and I haven't had eyelashes
for years? I burnt those wings off, pressed too tightly to the stove,

boiling potatoes. Everyone said I was all eyes like your baby
brother. All the ghosts are back when I'm cooking, the usual
blue-tongued fire of too many voices in the kitchen. Spoon
the pudding to set on the table piping hot. Like so, self-love

has to be measured out today, and not squandered. My sister out in the cornfields
was a nun and she had a PhD in chemistry. Myself, sometimes
Elizabeth's a queen. Or I'm the flapper, Betty Boop. I come from a long line
of women willing to increase or diminish vanity to taste: *With pearls or without?*

When I fell, I called the fire department, and lay
back on the floor, and those men, and there were two
of them, they swooped me up. Imagine whirling, in dancing
shoes, from one man's arms to another: *O to be myself again!*

## Mary Delany

Who invents the word *botanize* in a hasty letter,
a long letter because she didn't have the time to
self-prune. Leaving behind shellwork, needlework,

paper silhouettes, and after her favorite husband died
when she was in her seventies, she made collages of flowers
from minute mosaics of paper, egg white as glue,

laid against a black background, herself the blossomer
so accurate Erasmus Darwin praises Delany's careful scissors
as they ply. Sir Joseph Banks entrusts her with exotics.

Did you know you could become yourself
at seventy? So much so that Carl Linnaeus, great name-giver of
over twelve thousand plants and animals, draws from her mosaics

archetypes, specimens, new binomial names. This was well before
feminism, beyond its waves. Whose bits of paper, like the small-leaved
linden, dramatize our fates in flowers, "married females barren,

concubines fertile." Who paints with watercolors
each strand of paper so small you couldn't touch
it apart from your fingernail sticking to it, and arranging what looks

like a painting from afar, not separate pixels. Who, when she began to lose sight,
wrote poetry to her flowers, remembering the "solitary hours"
they shared. She saw in her mind the shadowy light on her favorites

even if she lost some of the Latin names like the second glove
in a dim, narrow closet. I was even younger
than I was, and for the first time away from home,

drinking SoCo in Soho, walking home arm in arm with friends
singing Madonna. Yes, I stole a piece of stem or stamen
from the special collection I'd lied to see and touched

and touched and then shook till Delany's egg-white glue let go.
Was it Winter Cherry or some Medusa web of stargazer
lilies paper collage, 1770s? I don't know where the scrap's now, stolen for what.

## Beneath the Waves

for my father

How we got into my father's top-secret submarine, I don't know,
but the bunks had felt-cutout everything, pillow small as the gold circle moon,
then the blanket as the green rectangle door, a story open
as no one is open in real life, to so many flatnesses trying out mezzo-sopranos,
and instead of my father disappearing for months under the waves, I came too.
Like the Beatles' yellow submarine.
Except here, you can take a three-minute shower between the hours of 2 and 4 a.m.,
where you're easily tugged from the light sleep
of those with torpedoes slung like a shoulder bag against the heart,
where you make overtime for the hardships of living in a vessel

that survives six months at sea, more than any person could bear
with nothing to do but triple-check in your dreams
the squiggles that press
so much furious cotton candy into the sky.
Nothing for me to do at fifteen
but assume I invented eternal damnation
though anxiety traveled like a loose-collared hand-me-down
smelling like an Alanis Morissette music video,
hips cutting into a blurry forest
to feel through what we ought to know but don't.

My father taught me about the world:
the navy would put a dead man in the freezer
before they'd come up out of the water early,
their mission undone. *Was he joking?* Though a helicopter and his submarine
kissed once to bring a dying man up to see another day.
*Why him? Why me?* My father was unreachable in the water:
all the W's and how's were the diffident high school journalist's aching
to know someone's—what was the word I used then? *Real inner thoughts?*
*The real you? The person you talk to when you talk to yourself in the shower?*
Questions of questions that froze forever at the invisible bars between minutes.

## With Palliative Care

The body you ferry is the ship you're ferrying, a walking
fermenter, a pacing host of fantastically fervent contagion.
You drift three steps toward life-extension, one back toward
self-extinction, and our unnamed friend, call her Beauty,
aged out of the modeling industry at twenty-five; call her
Truth. You know the interior stubbornness of blood-flecked
urine so unwilling to drop it was like labor. The calcified agony
in your kidneys screamed with pebbly multiples until laser-shot,
stone-agony rained down. You're up to so many poems, still not ready to
rain down the *Collected*, one more book to write down dying.
The body disintegrates, falls like ash. I know we came from maternal
pinholes of light that we'll fade back into. If illness is
a kind of intimacy, I feel closer to you now, with the taste
of arterial blood in my throat, how it colors the word-handsels
I sent like roses, myself I sent nearer than the smell of blossoms
in your room, more blossomy than death. I know you over wet leaves
and saltmarshes. You never lull a moment to listen to the body sick,
the body poor, but those flare-ups want to talk more,
and more frequently now like childhood memories of women's voices
you thought were gone. A word from a good friend, also in pain,
is the sticky salve of your cursing breath, thinking this is the end like ice chips
the size of coins on your tongue. "I am idle and I am in a whirl in one feverish world
while dreaming in a thousand others." Are we lit within, bacteria-consumed,
hotter to the touch, redder, brighter, more alive scribbling to each other, of
"the last oozings hours by hours"? A carriage door of hands surprising
dusk with flowers, some new news, if only for a moment—your nearness
nearer than the taste of the last days of summer: the jouissance of "butterflies
who live but three summer days—three such days with you I could fill
with more delight than fifty common years could ever contain."
I saw the champagne butterflies whirl up into each other, effervescing
the way we're laughing, the way we're talking far too far over the last threshold.

## Keatspeare

On the one hand, Keats sleeps entombed in his own monastic mind.
In a dark seminar room, my professor called it a "mind fuck." He, too,
was content in his own rich imaginative world, not even room for his sisters
during childhood, or his father's funeral when he was in Europe,
but there was his mother's "Century of Pain" he was around for, mostly.
In light of Keats and his personal biographer, my teacher,
I don't know what I think about the early detection of autism. Some radio doctor says
the twenty-month-old just needs convincing that mommy's mind
is just as interesting if not more so than his own. That the shaking
of the one toy in the exact same way should become a social enterprise
where the fixation can unclench, certain demands relax
to togetherness, to being-with. All along, the autistic child
"caught early" can adapt to new rituals enforced: she must scare,
mouth agape, eyes locked, a shiver through her chest,
to the sound of her name in Mommy's throat.
*Is her imagination as comforting, as ecstatic as mine?*
The child must stop right now to the rush of her mother beside her
on the carpet to the choke-hold of the mother's gaze,
the mother-mirror, the first voice, the first process of becoming:
to sing now about an unevenly mangled pie made of cawing blackbirds,
a maid with her nose mangled, also unevenly, by these gaping blackbird
bills. All this follows eye contact, which is why eye contact
must be avoided: what do they need you to see with them?
What do they need you for now? A girl eaten by a captor-wolf in
bed—the grandmother must be dead, too: am I already dead inside?
Are the storybook voices what Keats called "The great Bore with his anecdotes,
the flummery"?

On the other hand, Keats says, "The poet has no self;
he is continually in for—and filling some other Body,"
a Woman just the same as the Sea, Man, Sun, Moon.
The "gusto" of the mother, then, "foul or fair," the poet mops up.
The child with autism culls a self from self-stimulation,

as the bend of the playground skull at recess functions to prevent encroachment
from others, to allow absorption in sky and cloud. Keats laughed,
"here lies one whose name was writ in water" engraved on a headstone, for Plato
who thought poets liars on sensory overload, loquacious and "false as water," always
changing form. It was Keats obsessing over what position he dreamed Shakespeare
to be in writing: sitting, standing, or slouching with the left arm draped,
resting across the head, or fist clenched in that "and-on-he-flared" face
Keats is posthumously famous for, or lying on the ground, while drafting the soliloquy,
you know the one, the always-famous-before-it-even-was speech.
Now how is it that Keats's curiosity about how Shakespeare
aligned his words to his body posture outlasts the taste of that
moment's Hamlet. Is it odd of Keats to want to know the figure a man cuts,
"sorry-in-love" being the worst cut? Is he taking apart a toy text?
To want to be inside Shakespeare's spine as it coaxes that ten-beat line out of the preceding one,
to know whether he walked in circles, cursing, or caved in on himself,
or had his best thoughts first like Ginsberg, or vexed thought in the bathroom,
or while racing, not walking, away from someone he owed money to.
Filling poet, teacher, student, mother, child,
this business of wanting to fill the body of another—
to see how the body composes, while decomposing.

## Pebbles and Bones from Natural Places

for Paul O.

Fast drinker with no Zen tea left in the square-shaped purple mug, you're help in some rooms,
help-help in another kind of lighting with the flexibility of this: *Now how much time*

*do you have?* When you said that in your twenties, we were drinking two cups of tea, I never
thought you'd die at forty, fast after our teacher. All the tea urns, silver samovars, all on the

table, worth collecting, if not worth having. My younger brother is always ten years old to me—
there's the sideways but tall UPS package that he's knifing into and will hit an artery, the blood

on the phone. The voice saying, *I was trying to open my scooter.* Ezra Pound says somewhere a
girl asks her mother *if she can open the light.* My baby Scarlett's eyelashes, a frond of peacock

feathers, glitter open with light. Like the light of Henry-Moore-of-Pebbles-and-Bones-from-
Natural-Places fame. Outside, winter light rather than Irina on the Sun Porch,

Mary with Her Father, Moore Carving on Vacation in Italy. Winter with competing interests
such as earlier silence. What are you trying to remember? If it's not the riddle about fishnets,

then reliving stops along one line of the train, trainwreck songs, suicide on the train track,
by 7 a.m. the body's gone, the human hambone song, nursery rhyme, name songs,

someone's name whose father moves South, opens a frame shop, kills himself, time when
agency-existence isn't in jeopardy, when there's a touch-your-shoulder song

without your shoulder—and your latest shoulder,
if it's still lifelike as a good ear.

## The Chief Difficulty

However little reason he had to love his father,
he stood near the body, at the mouth of the vault,

on his bad legs "two hours, face bloated from
late paralytic stroke," playing the part of

"man that is born of woman," the chief difficulty. Born
a man "of few days and full of trouble."

Born unwanted, unfurled into more strife than should
fit into a few days. Near death himself, but here

to mourn his father, not himself, and wearing
a train five yards long, his best cloak, a wig,

the Duke of Cumberland could be a bride
or an orphan. He's a clouded leopard,

a burrowing owl in the glen,
a whistling duck with its face bent back in its feathers,

keeping a low profile in the grave scene, every
seventh man bearing a torch. Mourners with light.

There are mourners who kiss caskets
and who say they don't, but do sixty seconds

after the next guy, they're laying down a red rose
or a cigarette, kissing their hand, pressing it there.

On the other side of the plot, family to comfort
who seem in the least place to comfort. Try not to,

try not to remember someone dying as you're talking
just like this when one second later as in sleep he vanishes.

An important person cries upon entering
the picture of grief, swoons and wakes to smelling salts.

Horace Walpole, man of letters, tells us (not thinking of us)
that one mourner, busy looking around

to see who didn't show, busy "mopping his eyes,"
doesn't look where he's going, feels the chill of marble

through his shoes, steps on something soft, carpet-like,
keeps standing there on the Duke of Cumberland's train.

The duke, the son, the chief mourner, the orphan,
sinking with heat, trampled, weighed down, freezes.

I wait with a body, too afraid to move.
I'm in my car, beside a man thrown from his motorcycle.

In a pile-up of traffic, I can't not wait next to him. Isn't
this already enough of watching, looking down

at bodies this summer at midsummer: two best friends
lost a parent; or, those two sisters, their glasses embedded

in their skulls, the car in the tree, a mile from home;
then the friend I learned Latin with—they let us teach ourselves

and sit out of Spanish, to quicken dead poetry—
the person I showed poems to, the guy with the YIELD sign

nailed to his bedroom wall, my friend who overdosed.
I threw away the whole yearbook we coedited

except for his note to me with Sandburg quotes,
some Latin, all in blue-green marker like wet meadow grass.

What are we yielding to if we don't know we're yielding?

But this motorist is here, below me, robot-esque in leather,
so I will mourn him the highway out of here.

# Julia Flyte

Charles is Julia's but only after her brother Sebastian,
who meets Charles at Oxford, has him.
Sebastian, wasted, throws up in Charles's first-floor

open window. The next morning jonquils, hundreds,
alter the first impression. Out of one bouquet
a note to come to lunch at noon,

signed by Sebastian and his silly teddy bear,
who beg forgiveness not for drinking too much,
but for how various the drinks were.

At lunch there are plover's eggs to start,
a passionate clip of "The Waste Land" by a guest
stuttering on the balcony. When Sebastian has Charles

many more times at his real home,
Brideshead, mansion turned playhouse,
chapel turned gallery turned actual

fortress, the Flyte who stands out, threatening,
is Julia, with her lap dog burrowing
in the dark place that is warm

and loved because of her childless marriage,
vacuous adultery, airy religion, and the toy breed,
called a baby, a flirt, a thing.

It's as if Charles is already lighting Julia's
cigarette in the car and trembling. Already whispering
Charles Ryder and Julia Flyte to himself.

Riding, flying, because the atheist
and the fallen Catholic are about to,
like the orange time ball, crash atop a kind of steeple

in the sky, that drops down the spoke at one
in the afternoon, and several ships fire to give
clockless mariners everywhere something to go by.

# Discoveries

—taken from the letters of Sir Joseph Banks (1743–1820), British explorer, natural scientist, and litterateur

*1.*

Vexed by a full bladder, halted & hoping that urine would prattle on eventually, & this line of talk and life as usual, I lie cramped in an overturned stagecoach, pinned with my sister Sophia, her head bloodied, later dressed with lint with ardent hope, & then she just dies. All I could think was waterfalls, wanting to piss. Now who's better versed than me in the course of nature: a life of calamities, low spirits, the fear of Dissolution, & the Oblivion of an untimely grave?

I write, My dear Sir, my Lady Charlotte, Doctor Benjamin Franklin, mad, mad, mad King George, my poor turtle made into turtle soup, the *HMS Endeavour* mid-Endeavour Strait, Bligh, Reverend, Falconer, Hunter, incarcerated Flinders in too small a vessel upon too long a voyage, Ann in command of a ship, Fourth Earl of Sandwich, the Royal Society, God, an Unknown Correspondent, to whom shall I write & who will call upon me tomorrow morning early enough, liberate my mind from this grief journey?

I wish my sister outlived me: her petticoats full of books. But my Love of Botany continues, affording amusement, putting mistakes right, showing a Lady how to dry not the difficult Mosses just yet, but the wild sentimental Forget Me Not, & continues to be the subject matter of warm correspondence on my table before breakfast but not cream tea to get straight to:

*2.*

The ship's natural enemies are rats, mice, & cockroaches. Constantly look to see if the bark & young buds are getting gnawed like a virgin's neck. Treat the deck with a powder of white hellebore root mixed with bread dust & a little sugar—to kill them. A powder for getting a woman to love you, or love you more, or to bring her back, or to rule her, I'm looking for a folklorist in the New World to tell me, a woman.

3.

Large as a middling lamb, with a tapering tail long as the body, a quadruped, one of few we caught. Its coloring, dark mouse. Ears ovate-oblong. In the rocky, bad ground they hop deftly, easily beating my greyhounds. I've brought the female's skins, all three skulls, & a wash drawing of the skulls. We sailed in part to witness the Transit of Venus: here she is, the pretty-faced Kangaroo with white markings sweeping her cheekbones.

4.

A second time the natives threatened us: fire thrown out of reeds, long pikes, & small weapons of polished stone. I struck two warriors low down upon their legs, now so lame as to walk with great difficulty. At least four Maori men died, thus ending the most disagreeable day My Life has ever seen. Black be the mark for it & heaven send that such may never return to embitter future reflection. Discoveries from the Voyage: 1,000 Species of Plants that have not yet been described by any Botanical author.

5.

You seek cures for barrenness. Many will pay a large sum for a Male. Practitioners say they will render the shape of the Uterus more fit for conception than Nature had done: irritating it by Injections. After the injection, and a thimble of rich milk made from crushed soybeans & a taste of the fruit of a peach tree begun by almond seeds, have very slow sex, her toes raised like spindles afterwards. As for me, chaste garden walks, invariable, inconstant sex with a friend boarding through a rainstorm—playing botanist with the butterfly mounting pins, I know nothing of fathering but for letters that swoop, warm, autumnal. I can't accept the Theories—so many careless points—in the dissertation Mr. Lung forwarded me. Some should stick to the fetuses of whales in casks of malt spirits; the puffin & the murr—if they are larger, take off their skins with the head and feet still on.

## Fringe Festival

How the bulldog barks at every bird it sees,
leaving its game. Once he crashes through the window
onto the balcony to defend against

the parade of installation artists
marching in the Fringe Festival, and breaks half a pane to see
the bicycle decorated as a lobster, scuttling.

How Lonnie Glosson's harmonica says back to him, "I want my mama,"
and then, "I want a drink of water." He plays with his talking harmonica
"Why Don't You Haul Off and Love Me?"

When you sit alone, you hear that teenage girl again, saying her nerves
hurt. You swear you hear the quietest shudder in your body,
from fear, unyielding self-abasement, disgust, or the cold,

but don't see the flash which would have been a dead giveaway.
Your dog doesn't even look at the three chickens in the yard,
not the one with zigzag zebra stripes and a rooster's cockscomb.

Burton says the causes of melancholy are God,
parents, and old age. With all the kinds as diverse
as the sections of the head opened, cut up.

# 5.

# Hysterical Ballads

## *Preface*

Whatever, Wordsworth: Dear Reader is the Poet. The poet is above all a reader. Poetry is nothing more than hysterical citation. A love affair with the bust I'm drawing in college: I've made too soft the edges, and my teacher says, "Hannah's having a love affair with marble." I thought it looked like someone I knew, truth be told, and started breathing that adultery into it. Only I was eighteen, and that was never going to happen anyway: he was with an actress whose knees locked, but she was working through it. The text calls to you, like T. S. Eliot's hyacinth girl. Her hair is wet in the rain, but the poet there isn't speaking, maybe isn't even alive, so you may as well jump in and play her. In college, I read *The Waste Land* footnotes all in a row, and not the poem; then the notes before the poem, deep breath, apple, tea, poem; then the notes, back and forth, with the poem; then one more time, back to the notes, just the notes. When someone I trusted said the notes were a joke, I felt like there was nothing else I would part with more willingly except maybe my life, like Hamlet, melancholic, manic reader four hours in the halls where Ophelia will be loosed any moment now. I still read *The Waste Land* the way I first read it when I first "heard, half-heard in the stillness" of the bed in the room all those voices in the poem Eliot almost called *He Do the Police in Different Voices.* The working title that is not working.

The legacies of Eliot's faux anti-confession, on the one side, and of American confession and the cult of personality, on the other, still argue like siblings within me, and make me ashamed of the feelings in the heart of the heart of my poems, but I've redoubled my efforts to express and erase myself in one gesture. The poet-reader-self speaking through intertextuality, affect, whim, touch, memory, one more thought, one last thought, and that's all I'm going to say, whatever. It's like you're a schoolgirl and the teacher asks you to read your work, but you'd rather read the poem that inspired you or the eight things you were thinking about before you wrote it and the person you thought of after you wrote it, and then after all that when no one's listening, quick, bullet-point-like, paraphrase your stupid shit, explain the double meaning of the title. There were years I kept my coat on in the house: "Take your coat off, take your coat off." I was sweating, I was too skinny, I wasn't eating, I was awkward like the line halting before something happens and the next line can begin, something else major and the next stanza can open. I love my feelings inside other people's poems, and I can't talk about mine without the books I was reading at the time, soundtracks of feelings.

The subject is obsession, not particulars. The speaking voice is historical, archival, confessional. The speaking voice is personae. The snake tongues of Medusa rattle nonsense out of the cranium into metrical prose. The subject is neediness. Urgency. The you is more often an I. Everything is a mask, including language, why Oscar Wilde said what he said about masks and the truth, and you don't honestly want to hear that again. The subject is what my mother said all the time, "Why make mountains out of molehills?" I am sometimes talking to myself to make the past immediate. Or I'm having a moment with someone from another century and we're laughing hysterically over pleasure and pain.

My entry into poetry began with two relatives in a psychiatric ward. Which brought about my first period, at fourteen. I had to walk to get tampons. I slept on the floor near my father's bed. The poems I wrote had nothing to do with my fear of language inverting itself, hysterical prophecies, pre-elegiac suicide notes, pain I would know at the loss of my family. I wrote poems about unrequited love, as all teenagers do—why Keats says being sorry in love is the worst figure a man can cut. I was grimacing in self-pity and self-aggrandizement, magnetizing the voice inside my head to my RSVP blue pen, and I was bowing to my bed, lined paper against the starchy comforter, and then I stood at attention to receive a finished poem: my first poem! I was so serious about tapping into emotion, I didn't want to waste my emotional energy on music so I didn't listen to any. Something in me wanted to work on poetry, I needed silence, a locked door. Turn off those terrible lyrics, clichés, and roses. I don't know how long this lasted before it didn't.

You never have to go too far to seek out pain or pleasure. They say everything you'll need as writing fodder has already happened to you. Don't miss the meaning. Have the experience; go back for the meaning, and pastiche it all together, this lifetime and that, this text and today, the weather and your children talking, this question and this other iteration, the painting and your anxiety. Everything you'll need's already happened, including all you've read up to that point. Amelia Bedelia even (the poor white who refuses to do any sensible work for the rich white folk), absurdist puns and jest, even, resulting in what one always wants to do: mix and create, be startled by your own chiming oven.

Why look for shepherds and boy idiots and thorns and mad mothers and whatever else when you're your own best neurotic, sleeping shepherd boy, the sheep's in the corn, the inconsolable grief of child loss, the heaving thing giving birth but herself not yet born. And then, there's the pangs of lovesickness, the spectrum of the mood ring experienced in a moment, excess, silence, thoughts of death, suicide, female desire. The left hand doesn't know what the right is doing. Poetry is you take this thing over here and you take this thing from way over here, and you bring them together, against each other. And if you care, if you're milched with loss, then it will all work out; otherwise, there's no exigency. No one cares unless you're Barthes holding up the fucking image of your mother, the Winter Photograph, and then all the work makes perfect sense. You have to find your punctum. It's usually to do with mothers.

One kind of son throws a whole cabbage at the chandelier. The same kind takes the medicine doll to the doctor's home, points to the doll's body where his mother's sick. My son threw a book at me tonight. Then he put two pumpkin seeds to my mouth like extra communion. My daughter, the baby, turned the pages of her board book, ate the spine, the corners. My other daughter, the oldest, read the words, "emerged from the darkness," and she knew, intrinsically, my pleasure in hearing her own voice emerge from the darkness, like that, in a turn of phrase, from the back of the car. I couldn't have expected it from out of nowhere, that language.

*1.*

Cross-legged on a hill that's snaggy with roots, my
plaid skirt, purple and gold, butchered with red rapiers,
I'm etching with a paperclip on a black page
the white eyeliner wisps of the dandelion. No,
irate quills. I'm sixteen, I've read both Cranes, I know too much to address
the universe, who has no "sense of obligation" to me; and I'll never
fabricate my own "myth to lend to God" like the Brooklyn
Bridge across time, space.
I would have said *As if* then, or, my favorite, *Whatever.*
The dandelion and I don't ask too much of each other,
misrecognition is attentive enough. The asterisk
on a stalk fragging everything it loves, a flower
spreading out its sensations: my heart, that detonating kaleidoscope,
when I'm on my period. With my mother, but do I
bring it back to her, or does she send me like that, into school with
what she said, "It's like you can't even stand yourself?"

2.

William Cowper's the stricken deer on the highway,
entrails, foamy guts, but pre-crow, splayed heeled feet in prayers
muttered the night before, open-mouthed and going over the days
like a shark tooth you show your brother. Slammed, trucked over
when you hear the dream's calling you a *thee*
in a tunneling dark between rooms, a corded tin,
or did you hear, *A Happy New Year to Mr. Cowper,*
*it will find you working on your Homer!?*
It's easier to work on Homer than yourself.
My aunt said we drank Emotional
Iced Tea, that she, too, dwelled in
the absolute heights of emotion. Her cursive notes,
nearly every word underlined like hangman letters.
My brother made it feel like if you came out of the closet,

you leapt into your own unmarked grave.
Almost bereft of brother to suicide attempts,
the night he took all those sleeping pills and Benadryl,
he'd given me his prized possession, so I guess I should have
known, but didn't, like when he said, "What's the one crime
you can't be prosecuted for? Murder of the self, haha."
He gave me a collection of books so sticky
with lip gloss sheen in patent red leather, a lame Reader's Digest
set of classics, ugly as a church lady's purse. Those books
I couldn't read: they played scattered ghosts to his fantasy coffin.
Brother and sister, theologians of Calvinist suicide ideation.
He told me the answer to my "Who Am I?" essay was
"a damnable wretch." I wrote the essay. I am still
trying not to believe him. Red tulips, empty townhouses.

3.

Obsession ad # 81, where a piece of hair skirts
across her eye across the bridge of her beautiful nose—
not that a broken nose would be bad; people used to roll lint,
make other bandages. She is whatever you want,
even a little boy. Kate Moss, no shirt, breasts like targets.
Hippy hair, part down
the middle. She is the skeleton
in many photographs, both the woman's skeleton
and the child's at her ankle.
With degrees in Egyptology and paleopathology,
a woman knows for certain a third of the dead are young.
A child's skull has legions in the eye sockets.
Green eye paint is good for fighting infections;
it's because of the malachite.
That's nice in the way

the queen's boyfriend, Leicester, placed his wife's hat back on,
having thrown or paid to have her
thrown down her own steps. Did the woman tick a little
like the bird between steps near the bottom of the Duomo?
Not the only motive to move,
pain. You'd run much faster, farther,
from art, beauty just another kind of pain,
why Wharton says we run from the opera
faster than we flock there in carriages,
New Yorkers fleeing, especially
those who arrive late to begin with, Archer
with a name like Archer. He's
so messed up, he's like a tree the boys
use its own branches to hit it with.

4.

It gets better on its own: everything
but not the wild grief of the inconsolable mother.
Someone carries a tray of coffees.
There's no food. A hand from somewhere caresses the woman's cheek.
All her relatives and friends, even a small child, become her:
geographical faces, heavy-lidded scraps of eyes,
skin pleated, ploughed, and crosshatched with crow's feet,
smile lines, barred foreheads, wavy and wrinkled riverbeds.
Men's faces so close they could be kissing.
Three men link arms like girls hoarding the sidewalk
with laughter. Faces from sepia ink to bundle of wheat carry the same burden
as if you could go to bed as yourself
and then wake up as her. Everyone looks the same when someone dies.
Muted rupture, feigning the wild sublimity that comes with a wake.

The Hyacinth girls are sort of mourning, sort of
not. Pressing the inside of each other's wrists
with hot cigarettes, until the skin has its own ash center.
They have matching nipple rings, left breast,
matching velvet hats, and when they go to the bathroom together,
they're either doing coke or they're lipstick lesbians surely,
but they entreat men to give all kinds of free therapy
for their public outbursts. The attentive talk is enough,
nothing done: no deathbed conversion, no public crying, minimal
cheeses. They are writing poems and planning a dog tattoo. Who's to say
what's kindling? There's the ninety-day yoga challenge at U Street, there's pink
and red and blonde highlights around the corner, four pairs of shoes each
at Dupont, vodka and raisin diet, time to perfect emotion at
the bar Asylum, one of them is in the air with the bouncer.

5.

Sheer dread. Why Henry Moore keeps up
with Henry Moore: turning the Madonna into knee, elbow, oval
with points, row of sleepers, all inventions
on the level of Reproductive Physiologist Howard's work
with panda births or on the level of the penlight in the month-old
giant panda's mouth like yours.
Once, my mother thought it was the thunder of the end of the world
when it was just the garbage man. She said nothing,
then the ambulance came, and I thought they'd break
her shoulder. I was crying. In days, she was fine,
meds can activate psychosis.
I thought my baby was surely dying
while I was in the shower. It was a phantom cry. The baby
sound asleep, tucked like a fluffy comma on the crib.

# Alice Walker's Couch

This is how it starts: a woman slashes her mirror with taped quotes,
the manifesto-mottos of feminist writers, who themselves were left
by a lover or two, and who, anticipating more dings to their barely resolved
rejection-complex, say this, no more: to divest oneself of the need to be loved
is the beginning of self-love, and we know loving oneself is,
à la Wilde, "the beginning of a life-long romance."

You don't want to love yourself, hardly even like yourself, all that long, do you—
But what to do with the need to love, the flailing, winged other-side of the same fish,
is a moot point, because rooted in the same desperation to be texted back,
to be invited twice, in person, to the same function, to flit a little higher,
vainglorious with your own generosity in bringing nice alcohol
to the party. The womanist writer says you need a couch, not a bed: her one piece
of relationship advice. And the word rings out, is heard,
even by those without any kind of couches at all;
by those with character couches that make enormous dust clouds
when slapped in the chest, and unheeding all who sit there,
cat-claw lacerated, uneven slopes of slinky-popped springs;
and by the elderly who wait there, in reupholstered, poufy sofas, for the phone.

And by all the eyesome twenty-somethings, barely with-it enough
to acknowledge all bonding occurred with haste and while wasted,
not even amounting to one delicately bruised ear,
barely self-mocking enough to call their daybeds their sole couches.
Yet, once in these rococo chaise longues, you talk with someone three hours
straight, and, ignoring the woman nearby smoking with the aid of a carrot,
you reach certain understandings only in the flesh.

Walker might have found the hope chest the most couch-like surface of youth.
While the cedar got heavier each move,
with my brother heaving my bachelorette one-room furniture like a pallbearer would a coffin,
I turned my hope chest into my only couch, firm like a sleek memorial bench in a dog park,
filled only with pugs and French bulldogs, collars pink,
where you could say nothing alone together in anniversary-level telepathy.

On one side of you, a wreathed donkey pulls a tourist-carriage, decorated in
purple and white roses; the other, a purple party bus is a dancing boom box.
I live between the antique carriage house, swampy with hosed-down manure,
and the widest road to the French Quarter. My daughter sleeps
with the house ablaze in party-bus disco lights, erratic lyric blasts,
and the quickening clippety-clops of donkeys at the end of the day.

## Virginia Woolf in the Air

Another wet afternoon, Woolf's burying a sparrow
in the wet dirt: flowers, song, dusk, the whole thing. Another
century, Woolf's in the pre-sunset sky all the way in
Cape Canaveral, all the birds dodging a blitzy rocket launch.

Forget the names of progress, modernity: see the rocket spit
and foam hammering birds into forced nosedives. Is
the predator the whole sky? No time for glances back
at the wounded atmosphere shaking at the rocket's gavel

until the birds hit concrete, dirt, grass, beach, sea, wherever
like hot wax pressed over the letter's dry mouth.
The engineers ask themselves exactly like this:
*Why are all these birds committing suicide?*

Someone thought of setting up the launch beside a pool—
no joke. The water to muffle and pad the sky like blankets
and a small sofa pillow inside the jarring center of the snare drum.
A pool deescalating the homicidal, vibrating air pressure in the sky

desensitizing the instinct for plummet, so the sky
won't rain down suicidal birds scared shitless, so the rocket's
not so much of a shock, so the bird will soar out, far from here,
but it won't drop dead from the sky, heart whirling.

The engineers had to count the dead
to find the winning idea. Did you know water could stroke fear
down like that like your therapist saying, "sniff the roses then blow
the candles out, breathe in, out." My brother folded a suicide note,

laid it over the butter knives, slammed the utensil drawer,
but my father, the engineer who raved at rocket launches,
who calculated the secret arcs of missiles from submarines to
nameless shanks of beaches, found the letter before it was too late.

To reassure me, my brother said there's no cure:
there are coping skills. Brown pelicans
of the oily wetlands know there's only so many spills
Dawn soap can cut through in nature.

Or there's nothing but the glare-blast of
morning, and it's Clarissa Dalloway who
finds out she's for-sure sick,
but goes out anyway in search of buckets of flowers.

The burning clarity of Dalloway plunging
into her contemplations
one London summer day
into the flower shop's mists, and into the

afternoon in the privacy of her bedroom
where an old flame appears, sets down
the pocket knife to kiss her hands
mending a dress she's always mending.

# Unfairhopelessness, Alabama

Oxygen-poor bottom-dwellers whirl up from the depths to the cusp
like seaweed spread after a hurricane: needlefish, bay whiffs, shiners, juvenile
catfish, eels, shrimp, blue crab, croaker, spot, flounder. No breath left in these fifteen

miles of water so all oceania stills with the languor of a teenage girl's summer sleep.
The Fairhope and Daphne stretch of oxygen-starved Mobile Bay
is immobile. The waves dead, gray, and thin as wartime economy paper

they'd print novels on, those ripply pages so cheap they tear from your humid page-flips.
Without enough oxygen to "see to see," sea life flops into the trident, pitch-fork stab,
the haul-heave onto beach, tub, truck. Those trucks with the chrome ballsack

the road dribbles. Multiple generations of fishermen slept right on the pier
last night, covering it like catfish in tight quarters, washing their faces
in a bucket of bay water before bed, then waking to their catch.

Fishermen call this Jubilee, the few chances a year before sunrise
when plants eat light for air. They get away with truckloads
of fish too tired to panic. Part of me wants to think they won't die,

that the sunrise will save or at least resurrect them. I smelled the dead all over.
We called it Unfairhopelessness. Ourselves ecopoets who couldn't breathe,
one of us pregnant, who couldn't dream of peeing

in this ocean. Here, it's rank with life, no death
at Jubilee, where seeing's as good as reaping. Where the fish-who-got-away tales
don't exist, where the water's edge burns with anchovy stench,

a blue crab blows bubbles. An eel who buried itself tail-first
into the wet sand, mouth agape,
is rooting around, guessing *Where's a life?*

## After Brueghel's *Children's Games*

A humming girl rolling a hoop with a stick and her knee
doesn't notice someone in her path:
the boy inflating a bladder after pitching two at his friend,
who turns them into water wings, swimming out.
The iron-monger's son collects foreign coins.
His hands behind his back, waiting for someone
to guess. The neighbor girl reaches for one arm.
His fist won't come undone, white-knuckled over
ducats: *It's here or you would show me.*

Older boys grab this kid's arms and legs.
On either side of the ledge, ramming him
while shaking lightly. They say they're making butter;
they whisk, churn, mash until pure cream peaks, seizes,
buttermilk gushes out. Six boys and the boy who is the butter.

The child-minder calls them back inside, pretending they're hers
when the sun slides behind the fence where the harvest is,
but forsakes her own name, Hannah, story of the barren, biblically
drunk and actually drunk wailer, begging for a son though
she'll have to leave him forever at the temple where he'd wake
to high cries, sobs, God's, at night. She could wait for a reticent answer

only so long, always inside her the child hugging herself to sleep
so no one loots her soul, except when sneezing, without sentry,
when a bad spirit could enter your mouth. Worrying even in her sleep,
Hannah in the picture book you see pray-cursing at the scrolls
in the columns until promised a son to lift her hostile-uterus shame.
Just a teenage wife lying on the bed, holding her legs in the air
so the semen would work this time, and it does.
Don't you think she knows what's happening in her own body?

She couldn't resign herself to becoming another accepting,
slovenly wife, lowering her face to God, lying down in barren-default
defeat with a joke chance of aberrant luck: *If anything changes,
let me know,* but she could rend the heavens like angsty Monica
for a saintly son where you could die in peace, having made an
Augustine yourself. And Monica does, nine days after he confesses,
die like that. How our more pitiful double, Hannah, sorrowful, love-slain,

wounded from childbirth, doesn't want to do anything,
not climactically die or absent-mindedly tilt the ankles,
press bare heels into the floor, slightly rocking in the chair—
it's all too exciting for the hours of staring at the fire all night
until morning, partly dark like winter dusk, trying to collect herself
now that the baby is here, outside of her.
"Either you have children or you are a child": she is both.

## Every Time It Rains, a Requiem

My daughter would bring home
a hurricane that is only wind.
Born in New Orleans, she thinks hurricanes

will learn the art of conversation. Even small talk,
wind creaking the porch,
just sighing along, neighborly.

Remember when you destroyed
a sugar plantation, uprooted cane
like a bombed cemetery on the fringes of war?

You swept a sunflower seed near the sparrow knowing
it would clench the fatty tear fallen
from the face of the tall flower.

In the afternoon, you cooled the baby, born
in summer, wearing only a diaper
and ribbed white socks.

Forget the rage that speared
pickup trucks into trees,
or tried to swallow a city whole.

Once your rains were so tender
I saw a droplet in the shifting wings
of the fly on my windshield.

When you forget your lithium
and become this unmoored,
remember how it can't be good for you to talk that fast.

You didn't stop when she told God through the hole in the Superdome
to leave the baby with the week-old Pampers out of it. When a man with autism
yelled on his roof for the helicopter, and his daughter, who

never heard him yell in all her life, cried with her mouth open.
When a red pit bull gave birth in the storm and her whole litter drowned.
Now, every time it rains, the pink cottage, the white bathroom

become a wet manger on A. P. Tureaud Street,
and the dog's circling around, cramping,
thinking they need her warmth. They'll be there, just born.

## Hysterical Water

1.

*To Cause Conception*, take the whites of 16 eggs, beat well, and put them into the milk. Stir them well together into an ordinary silk with a soft firmness.

2.

"She felt the whole thing, she felt everything"—
They told me about my mother, who survived
the C-section she interrupted with "STOP!,"
because the person whose one job it was to numb
her belly from knowing it was being seared apart
had failed her. My baby brother went straight
to the incubator, swollen, swimming in three times
the pool of amniotic fluid. I visited him like he was
a strange sea creature at the aquarium, wanted to reach
my hands into the box but he was covered in wires.
Five months, the baby and I slept in my grandmother's
basement. I was eight, and, my mother, they said she was sick.
I used to wonder, *Did her hurt hurt? Like my hurt hurts?*
and now I wonder when did it not hurt, and has it ever stopped?

After all that, being cut open and sewn back in place, all without
anyone able to help the pain, because they're telling you
they can't stop in the middle of the section, and then your one gift
for all the suffering gets taken back. To hear a therapist saying you
had to take care of yourself first to take care of us. To feel your milk
coming in then drying up, no trembling uterine cramping
and shrinking back to size with each swallow your baby pulls
from your breast. Did they tell you to put cabbage leaves
in your bra and wait? How long does it take milk that's ready
to scramble back and never wet your shirt again at the sound
of any baby's cry or your husband's touch?

3.

*To Make a Woman Have Easy Labor,* half a handful of strained raisins, 12 figs, licorice sliced, anise seeds boiled in water, and take with a spoonful of almonds.

4.

When he was five, my brother said, when he found out they cut
my mother across her stomach to birth him,
and my mother screamed until she must
have nearly passed out, that he wished he was never
even born. Across the table, my father said, *We thought our childbearing years*
*were over, but you have brought so much joy to our*
*family*. I remember encircling my parents, us kids dancing, holding hands,
in wonder that in our home, there'd be those naked feet in a wad
of fat like a blowfish that no shoe would fit the helm of, and he'd
fall just perfectly on my hip as on my mother's, the toes
dangling like a blessing. A baby stepping into the inside-out panels
of our umbrellas on the carpet, tripping into the red, the blue
like a parachute against extinction. A baby to go in the middle
bench in the blue van that my mother said had leprosy,
but I believed in the magic of numbers, the new baby skin
for sad Naaman slapping the surface of the Jordan river, coming out
of the water, up for air, again and again. Is *again* the only request a child
ever makes? The ritual of joy is what Naaman engulfed in the air each
time he swooped out of the water like leaping salmon, times seven.

I never saw my father put down the Bible to eat, but he ended
his morning devotions to feed the new baby named not for one, but for
two gospels, John Mark. My brothers and I argued to
feed him the last bite off our plates, and begged him to "Come to the one
you love" when he began to walk. Now, John rides a motorcycle to 4 Times Square,
the only lawyer in our family after graduating in the top 3 percent. Today,
he ordered his couch and a piece of salmon to his apartment door,
and both came at the same time. Now taller than any of us by a head,
he once said we all treated him like he was the family pet, dragged on errands

and then treated. In kindergarten, he had the wherewithal
to correct the teacher: "It is E as in Einstein, not as in egg."

*5.*

To make "Hysterical Water to Cure Fits of the Mother," take 4 pounds of leaves of mugwort, a handful and a half of orange peels, 2 ounces of castor, and put 4 days in a vessel well-stopped. This is good to cleanse anything away after a woman is delivered of the child.

*6.*

It wasn't a simple postpartum depression like the slanted words
on the book with the blue cover and the slashes of white,
it had to be shock, disbelief, trauma, PTSD, grief, torture like almost dying
to have your wound wounding you with no help. If she could have had
the baby in the room with her like they did in England where they understood
this better. If there had been just women with the same thing there,
like Jewish women, who, when they feel like they're going to faint,
at the end of a long fast, pass around the orange or the lemon
studded with a clove, and they inhale it, one after the other. I think
my mother would have liked something like that, the way women
care for each other. I wish I knew her like that then, but I was only
a child and I thought the same thing would happen to me
because we had a matching sweater with red stripes
and a white Peter Pan collar, and we were the only girls
in the family. When the therapist asked her to draw how she felt,
she refused and said she wasn't creative, but then she finally dug in her mark,
"There! There's your dot!" and her therapist told her and then she told my father,
"There's a lot of meaning in that dot." I still think about that one little blue dot.
Punctuation, to puncture. She worried about my field trip on Sugarloaf Mountain
with my old shoes. I didn't have the right shoes for climbing. I was going to
fall off the mountain, and she kept dreaming about it.
She worried her baby wouldn't know her when she finally got him back at the house.
She worried the new baby wouldn't have records as nice

as the others. How she kept such records, even the first
tooth wrapped in tape, all the birthday cards from the first years, the welcome
posters, folded up in squares, from the day she brought us home.
When we came back together, there she was, again, the center of everything,
with a cubby of our childhood we'd climb back inside.

## Georgia Review Books

*What Persists: Selected Essays on Poetry from* The Georgia Review, *1988–2014*, by Judith Kitchen

*Conscientious Thinking: Making Sense in an Age of Idiot Savants*, by David Bosworth

*Stargazing in the Atomic Age*, by Ann Goldman

*Hong Kong without Us: A People's Poetry*, edited by the Bauhinia Project

*Hysterical Water: Poems*, by Hannah Baker Saltmarsh

*Divine Fire: Poems*, by David Woo